DEEP SOUTH PIANO

65p

Series edited by Paul Oliver

BLUES PAPERBACKS
Edited by Paul Oliver

In a series of monographs Blues Paperbacks examine important blues singers and musicians, local styles and traditions, subjects and themes, and the history and influence of this living music. The books are written by acknowledged authorities in the field and are of importance to enthusiasts of modern musical idioms, sociologists and folklorists, and students of the popular arts. Each book in the series is extensively illustrated with historic and recent photographs and printed ephemera, many previously unpublished, supported by maps, discographies, and bibliographies.

BLACKS, WHITES AND BLUES
Tony Russell
An historical examination of the complex relationship between the negro and white folk music traditions and the importance of the blues in both.

MA RAINEY AND THE CLASSIC BLUES SINGERS
Derrick Stewart-Baxter
A critical discussion of Ma Rainey, Bessie Smith and the 'classic' women singers of the 'twenties who first put blues on record and established its relationship to jazz.

SAVANNAH SYNCOPATORS – AFRICAN RETENTIONS IN THE BLUES
Paul Oliver
A re-examination of the problem of African elements in the blues and jazz, based on new research including the author's field studies in West Africa.

RECORDING THE BLUES
R. M. W. Dixon and J. Godrich
The story of the recording companies: their conventions, how and where they recorded the blues, and the singers they recorded.

CHARLEY PATTON
John Fahey
Himself a noted guitarist, John Fahey has made a textual and musicological examination of the music of Charley Patton, one of the most exceptional and influential figures in the history of the blues.

BLUES FROM THE DELTA
William Ferris, Jr.
This study of black folklore from the Mississippi Delta is devoted to the creative process in blues. The author has examined the unfolding of songs and verses in extended sessions, and has interviewed singers on their approach to music-making.

DEEP SOUTH PIANO
Karl Gert zur Heide
These researches into the rich blues piano traditions were conducted with the help of Little Brother Montgomery. This book examines the relationship of southern piano forms to blues and jazz traditions.

MEMPHIS BLUES
Bengt Olsson
An investigation and analysis into the factual history of the blues singers and musicians of Memphis, tracing their lives, the story of the medicine shows that recruited them and the uproarious background of the 'jug bands'.

DEEP SOUTH PIANO

The Story of Little Brother Montgomery

Karl Gert zur Heide

Studio Vista

*Produced by November Books Limited,
23-9 Emerald Street, London,
WC1N 3QL*

*Published by Studio Vista Limited,
Blue Star House, Highgate Hill,
London, N19*

*Text set by Yendall & Company
Limited, Riscatype House,
22-5 Red Lion Court, Fleet Street,
London, EC4*

*Printed by Compton Printing Limited,
Pembroke Road, Stocklake,
Aylesbury, Bucks.*

*Bound by Dorstel Press Limited,
West Road, Templefields, Harlow,
Essex.*

*© November Books Limited 1970.
Printed in England.
This edition is not for sale in the
United States.*

*Designed by Tom Carter.
House editor: Celia Phillips.
Copy preparation: John Leath.*

SBN 289.70028.0 *(hardbound)*
     289.70027.2 *(paperback)*

*All illustrations in this book are from
the collections of the author, the Series
editor, and private collectors; permission to reproduce other than for
review purposes must be obtained
through the publishers.*

Contents

Introduction 9

Brother

Kentwood 15

Away 18

The Forty-Fours 19

New Orleans 22

West Florida and Out West 27

Mississippi 32

Desdune 39

Chicago 42

Southland Troubadours 48

Post-War Appendix 55

Who's Who 59

Lyrics 93

Abbreviations 104

Discography 105

Index 109

Acknowledgments

This book was made possible by a great many experts and collectors. Anybody who had contributed to the relevant literature ran the risk of being read – and digested – by the one under whose authorship *Deep South Piano* is published. Communications with, and material from Paul Oliver, David Evans, Tom Stagg, and Dick Allen and the Archive of New Orleans Jazz proved to be most rewarding. Marina Bokelman, John Crosley, Bertrand Demeusy, Bill Ferris, Ray Flerlage, Ulrike Germeyer, John Godrich, Bob Groom, Friedrich Hachenberg, Christopher Hillman, John Holley, Bob Koester, Mike Leadbitter, Albert McCarthy, Jan Montgomery, Irene Morris, Simon Napier, Dick Raichelson, Al Rose, Tony Russell, Brian Rust, Francis Smith, Derrick Stewart-Baxter, Tom Stoddard, Chris Strachwitz, Berhard Uhle, Max Vreede, Gayle Wardlow and Pete Welding have not hesitated to give their encouraging help. Data from the contemporary Black American press was supplied by Walter Allen. The patience of Mr and Mrs zur Heide should not go unmentioned.

Personal contact with Oliver Alcorn, Danny Barker, Ishmon Bracey, Buddy Burns, Harold Dejan, Aris Gayten, Sammy Hopkins, Skip James, Walter Lewis, Howard Loach, Joe Montgomery, Henry Palmer, Luke Parmley, Frank Pasley, Judge Riley, Brick Roseby, Butch Roseby, Sunnyland Slim, Roosevelt Sykes, Annie Turner, Tuts Washington, J. Mayo Williams, Big Joe Williams and Sweet Williams was essential. Little Brother Montgomery was a friend in every way. Many cordial thanks to all of them! And probably to others not named here. Work on the subject will not end with the publication of *Deep South Piano*. Readers with comments, corrections, and additions and interest in further research are invited to write to Karl Gert zur Heide, 4993 Rahden, Lübbecker Str. 6, Germany.

Introduction

'Bro'r Montgomery? He been dead and gone a long time.' Ishmon Bracey hasn't seen Little Brother Montgomery in more than thirty years. In 1968, the black music scene of Jackson, Mississippi, has changed drastically: Tommy Johnson, its most influential blues singer and guitarist, had died in the 1950s. The famed show drummer, Joe White, is too senile to talk. The McCoy brothers, Charlie and Joe, are dead. Others, like Walter Jacobs and Rube Lacy, have just gone. The Chatmon family is scattered all over the country. Even Butch's Band has given up playing. And Ishmon Bracey and Tommy Johnson's older brother Ledell have turned their backs on the blues and hold the title of 'Reverend'. How should a local preacher, once a confrère of Tommy Johnson, know that Little Brother is very much alive up north in Chicago and still playing piano whenever there is a job?

Lack of factual knowledge favours the growth of legends, and information on black piano players from the Deep South is scarce. Literally thousands of them went unrecorded; still, an amazing body of their work has been preserved by various media. Eight years before the cabaret blues of Mamie Smith initiated the era of 'race' records in 1920, the first blues numbers were cut into player-piano rolls – presumably by established pianists who came in touch with the idiom through the publication of sheet music early in 1912. The year of 1897 saw the public appearance of ragtime which was, unlike blues and jazz, not essentially a Southern style. Twenty years later, five white instrumentalists from New Orleans brought a strange sound into a regular recording studio: the first release by the Original Dixieland 'Jass' Band featured their novelty interpretation of ragtime and blues. Jazz began to flourish, and within a decade numerous forms of genuine Afro-American folk music were issued in special series aimed at the 'race' market. Between 1926 and 1931 especially, these 'race' discs displayed a great variety of material, ranging from work songs to jazz, from blues to rags, from minstrel tunes to hokum stuff, from street cries to spirituals, and from sermons to boogies.

The complexity of this field impedes a satisfactory terminology. It seems necessary, however, to define some of the terms used here.

Although also performed on string instruments or by a whole orchestra, ragtime is associated with the keyboard. In the hands of accomplished Midwestern composers – black or white – it gained a European character in its melodic and harmonic structure, while it retained the rhythmic peculiarities of its Negro origin. Ragtime is marked by a stylised right-hand syncopation against a regular bass. Its three main left-hand techniques were transmitted to blues and jazz piano: stride, tenth, and walking basses.

The 'ragtime craze' ended with World War I, and jazz took over. Already it had been adopted and popularised by white groups – jazz left the realm of folk music. This way of playing 'hot' and 'fancy' and 'with plenty rhythm' emerged in the South, in black dance bands; its focal point was New Orleans. Ragtime master and jazz pioneer Jelly Roll Morton knew what he was talking about: 'Ragtime is a certain type of syncopation and only certain tunes can be played in that idea. But jazz is a style that can be applied to any type of tune.'

A jazz treatment would also be given to material stemming from secular and religious Negro singing. For a jazz musician, 'let's play the blues' first of all means to follow a rather fixed chord sequence of twelve bars. This formula has done much to domesticate – and stereotype – the blues, a musical language in its own right. Jazz sprang from urban surroundings – the blues came from the rural South. Jazz is communal music – a bluesman may sing and play to himself when 'the blues got him'. Contrary to jazz, blues is primarily accompanied *vocal* music.

The guitar always has been the favourite blues instrument, with the piano as a close second. The most distinct way of playing blues on the piano bears the label 'boogie-woogie'. In his superb analysis, Ernest Borneman clearly states that 'the boogie *is* the blues as far as melody, harmony, and length of theme are concerned'. The difference appears to be an often remarkable rhythmic diversity of both hands. Indeed it is the *ostinato* left hand of the player which holds the criterion: each beat – four to a measure in 4/4 time – is accented; this sets boogie apart from the oompah two-beat of stride. Slower tempi allow the use of triple inner-rhythm: the second note of the triplets is usually silent, and the third represents an unaccented afterbeat. Only duple rhythm can supply eight – accented, of course – beats to the bar, which should be notated in 8/8 time. In order to secure the same weight for each beat within a given chord, the fingers of the left hand either stay in one position (steady bass) or ramble up and down the keyboard in little steps (walking bass), varying position with each beat. Repetition of similar or identical figures produces patterns of four or eight beats. A walk can be 'doubled up' by inserting afterbeats in broken octaves. The 'Rocks' is neither 'steady' nor 'walking'; it is a triple bass which is executed by alternating two finger positions lying close to each other. The tenth and the 'Spanish' basses constitute borderline cases of boogie.

'I would say that boogie-woogie was the little bad boy of the rag family who wouldn't study', remarked music lover Roy Carew, witness of the early days. It is true that boogie owes more to ragtime than is evident, although it still has to be decided if the known blends can be regarded as pre-boogies, or are just hybrids. In his childhood, boogie certainly did not behave according to European conventions. The archaic manifestations of Afro-American music have a modal character and, in solo forms like boogie, no continuous metre. The latter is the result of linear thinking which disregards harmony in an academic sense. In groups of several players, this conception can lead to heterophony with strict metre; a good example is archaic jazz. Even when employing a certain chord sequence a 'country' bluesman would make the changes when he felt like it. Used to playing alone, he shows the tendency to corrupt the harmonic and metric scheme when performing with a band. 'He's breaking time', a trained musician would say.

The theme of boogie is the blues, some features derive from ragtime, and the rhythmic interplay of both hands can be traced back to African roots. But where and when did the first Negro play the blues with a boogie beat, and on which instrument? The Emancipation (1863) probably gave the impetus for the fusion of various vocal and instrumental idioms which led to the rise of the blues. It is open to question if the first piano boogie was anticipated by banjo and guitar styles with the insistent rhythm of players like Otis Harris or Garfield Akers. There is, however, no doubt that a number of guitarists cleverly adapted boogie piano techniques – among them Leadbelly, Robert Johnson, and Pet and Can.

The earliest reports hint at an origin somewhere between New Orleans and Dallas, Memphis and Houston, but Mississippi and Alabama also had strong boogie traditions. Anyway, the Deep South seems to be the heartland of blues, boogie, and jazz. 'Picking cotton' and 'picking guitar' is not too irrelevant an association, and perhaps another one can be established: between wood and boogie-woogie.

Above   *Shipping lumber in Tangipahoa Parish, Louisiana, c. 1900.*
Right   *Original Barrel House, North Halsted St., Chicago, 1968.*

Vast regions of the Deep South are wooded – Louisiana, Mississippi except for the Delta, and southern Arkansas. Here the main industry was, and still is, lumbering and wood processing. Towns grew around sawmills; some of their names show this: Electric Mills, Lumberton, Kentwood, Transylvania, Pineville. The resin of the pine-trees was distilled to turpentine. The different companies met their specific needs by instituting camps which would be moved when work progressed or a certain area had been exploited. The workers only left the camp, if at all, on weekends. For their recreation after long hours of toil there was a shack where they could eat and drink, dance and gamble. Similar places existed all over the country; they were known as barrelhouses, honky-tonks, and juke joints.

In the camps, the workers often supplied the music themselves, but now and then an itinerant musician dropped in – for example, Poor Joe Williams: 'I had one route I really liked to travel, and that was down around Mobile, Meridian, Electric Mills, Shuqulak, and on into Alabama. I'd hit all them turpentine camps down there. They'd have oxen pulling them two-wheeled carts dipping that turpentine. Boy, they'd have a wonderful time on Saturdays in those camps. When somebody like me went through there it was like the President coming there. They'd come from all over –

they hear talk of a man coming there with a guitar. They'd get real rough on Saturday night.'

Usually the camps were furnished with a piano, and it was customary to hire a player for a week or more. Many of these pianists were professional entertainers with a wide repertoire, but it did not help much to be able to sing the latest pop song, play tricky rags or tap-dance. 'That's all that was going for a barrelhouse – the blues', said Walter Lewis who first played Beethoven and then the barrelhouse circuit. The blues suitable for dancing – this description fits boogie-woogie. In his boogie folio Clarence Williams, a pianist more than twenty years older than Walter Lewis, handed down the perception that boogie developed in the lumber camps, logging camps, turpentine camps, and railroad camps.

On this subject, Roy Carew commented: 'I heard crude beginnings of it in the back streets of New Orleans, in these early years following 1904, but they were really back streets. More crude than Pinetop's efforts, such music never got played in the "gilded palaces".' It was only a step from the backwoods to the back streets of the cities, but a long way from the honky-tonks to Carnegie Hall. In the Deep South, pianos could be found in all sorts of places – sawmills, cabarets, roadhouses, churches, brothels, private houses, dance halls, country jukes, city tonks – and there was always someone who could 'tickle them keys'. It sometimes happened that the gospel pianist played in a hot dance style, that the barrelhouse man surprised his crowd with an operatic number, that the orchestral player stopped the dance with a slow blues. Through their very versatility, some of these pianists resist any categorisation – they were at home in jazz bands, honky-tonks, and cocktail lounges.

Little Brother Montgomery is one of these. A fair performer of hymns and pop tunes, an excellent traditional jazz man, a fascinating singer, Brother stands out as one of the greatest blues soloists and accompanists. Unlike most of his colleagues, he is relatively well known. What follows is his story; yet it is also the story of many others who travelled the same roads.

Brother Kentwood

The short-lived independent West Florida Republic (1810) covered a territory along the Gulf Coast between the Mississippi and Perdido River. Previously it had been claimed by France (seventeenth century), Great Britain (1763) and Spain (1782). Its portion west of the Pearl River was added to the state of Louisiana (1812), the rest came to Mississippi (1817) and Alabama (1819).

Remote areas were made accessible by the construction of railways. The New Orleans, Jackson and Great Northern Railroad, now part of the Illinois Central R.R. system, was built in 1852–3. This line opened up the primitive forests along the Tangipahoa River which empties into Lake Pontchartrain. Transport facilities meant economic development and increasing population. Already in the 1850s, an enterprising man from New Hampshire settled just south of the Louisiana–Mississippi border and established a sawmill and a brick plant on the railroad. The Amos Kent Lumber and Brick Company was the nucleus of a township which

Kentwood and Eastern Railroad Brooks Scanlon Company, Tangipahoa Parish, Louisiana.

Amos Kent Lumber & Brick Company: the saw mill with workers, Kentwood, 1902.

honours his name: Kentwood in Tangipahoa Parish, Louisiana. The very year that Kent left the scene for ever, our story began.

'Eurreal Wilford Montgomery was born in Kentwood, Louisiana, in 1906, April 18th, on a sawmill job by the name of Kent's Lumber Company', wrote Little Brother about himself. Both of his parents, Harper and Dicy Montgomery, were part Negro, part Creek Indian. As an ethnic unity, the Red Indians disappeared east of Mississippi River, but their blood remained: they mixed, unless they were expelled or killed, with the other under privileged racial group, the dark Africans. The Creeks ceded their territory around Fort Mitchell, Alabama, by the treaty of 1832. They went west via New Orleans where some of them stayed, among them perhaps the great-grandparents of Eurreal Montgomery. 'My father used to work in New Orleans, but they moved out to Kentwood, and I call that my home. He had a honky-tonk not far from our house over in Reeds Quarters. I'm one of ten children, five girls and five boys. From the oldest to the youngest they are Olivia, Willie, Leon, Aris, Ella, Eurreal, Joe, Willie Maxine, Willie Belle, and Tollie. They called me Little Brother from the time I was a baby, but at school they called me Little Brother Harper.'

The Montgomery family sang in the nearby Temple Chapel Baptist Church, and nearly all of them could play an instrument. 'Actually, my father's uncle had one of the first bands, Gonzy Montgomery and his Big Four Band. That was a regular serenade band, a dance band. He was out of New Orleans, came along with Bunk Johnson. His home was in Greensburg.' Harper Montgomery, nephew of multi-instrumentalist Gonzy, played cornet and his wife Dicy, accordion and organ; their oldest son, Willie, also tried the cornet.

Little Brother grew up with music. 'I used to fool around with bass tuba when I was a kid. My father bought a piano when I was three or four years old, and I began to play it at the age of five – you know, just on my own. All of my brothers and sisters learned to play later. I could make up pieces on the piano at the age of five or six. The first little things I started with was just two- or three-finger blues.' When Brother demonstrated this more than fifty years later, out came a twelve-bar blues of serene beauty. His left hand went up and down the chords with the 'Spanish tinge' associated with Jelly Roll Morton and Jimmy Yancey. 'My sister Aris can't play nothing else but that because it's easy to do. That came out of Louisiana.

'So from then on I just created simple things on my own until later on I got large enough and went to hear the real older people play – such as Son Framion and a guy named Ford. I heard men playing piano like Rip Top, Loomis Gibson, Papa Lord God, Sudan Washington, Leon Brumfield, Varnado Anderson, Ernest Haywood, one they called Reese, Clarence Seale, Bob Morton, Willie Anderson, Cooney Vaughn, and Jelly Roll Morton. I heard them because my father had a piano in our house where we lived, and these men would stop by and play because a lot of times they would be playing for my father at the honky-tonk. That gave me the inspiration of trying to be a piano player like those guys.'

Young Eurreal progressed quickly by listening to them and watching their fingers. 'They played quitely anything. The sort of music I heard around there was the same sort of music I'm playing now. Oh I played lots of numbers that were popular at that time, like *Mickey*, *Twelfth Street Rag*, *You Must Not Get So Musty*

'Cause Your Water's On – this is the tune we now call *Tin Roo Blues* – , *Get Over Sal* – they call this *Walkin' The Dog* – , *Tishomingo Blues*, and *A Long Way To Tipperary*. So you see I can do more than play the blues . . . '

Still it was the blues that Little Brother first of all tried playing. Most of the pianists drifting through Kentwood, or living there, featured a special blues. Varnado Anderson, Rip Top, Papa Lord God and Willie Anderson were among those whose blues Brother memorised. 'Cooney Vaughn played a blues he called *Trembling Blues*. And I learned another little blues from an old guy, he was a great piano player named Loomis Gibson. So later on up in the years he passed and I named them *Crescent City Blues* – that's New Orleans. But the real name of it was *Loomis Gibson Blues*. *Out West Blues*, that was Bob Morton's number. Leon Brumfield had one, they used to call it *Leon Brumfield Blues*. They come out of New Orleans, it wasn't Leon's; he must have learned it. You know what they did? Made the *Riverside Blues* out of it. And they stole the *Dippermouth Blues* from the *Bob Morton Blues* – they are strictly out of Louisiana.'

Little Brother's reconstructions of these pieces are spiced with boogie basses. 'We were playing all those kind of basses down there, way before ever it came out on records. I used to only play a walking bass with one finger then, but after I got up around twelve, fourteen I could double up and play with all of my hand. We called it Dudlow Joe.' This is confirmed by bass player Willie Dixon: 'They used to call boogie piano Dudlow Joes in Mississippi. I didn't hear it called boogie till long after. If a guy played boogie piano they'd say he was a Dudlow player. Later on guitars played boogie too.'

Away

Little Brother Harper was bound to become 'a piano player like those guys'. He undertook the decisive step very early in his life. 'I was only a seventh grade scholar when I left home.' He likes to reminisce about the musicians he knew and the stages of his own career, whereas he keeps his personal motives to himself. Laconically he reported: 'So I ran away from home at the age of about eleven and played piano for a living. I have been playing piano ever since.' The family ties were not dissolved for good, but at any rate he was gone – although he didn't yet venture beyond the borders of Tangipahoa Parish: Natalbany, Hammond, Ponchatoula.

'My first job was at a juke in Holton, Louisiana – for eight dollars a week, room and board. Mostly the people who got jobs in barrelhouses were piano players, and later on they would hire a drummer too. Singers dropped in all the time. During the week we played from about seven till ten or ten-thirty. They closed early so people could get to work. On Saturdays we used to start at nine o'clock and play all night long. They'd dance the Eagle Rock and the Grizzly Bear.' Little Brother met Joe Lewis, another piano player from the parish, and learned his blues, plainly titled *Joe Lewis Blues*. He also took up singing while in Holton. Fighting against the noise of the juke his voice developed a piercing quality with a tight vibrato, the trade-mark of his vocals to the present day.

Nearly two years of barrelhouse practice gave him enough confidence to leave the relative seclusion of Holton. 'I moved on to Plaquemine, Louisiana, where I played five or six months for a fellow called Tom Kirby at a cabaret. That was ten dollars a week room and board. Then I left there and went to Ferriday, Louisiana, and played for Ed Henderson at Henderson's Royal Garden for fifteen dollars a week and room and board.' There he made friends with Long Tall Friday and Dehlco Robert, both honky-tonk pianists working in Louisiana and Mississippi. 'Me and Robert was playing at the Royal Garden. Sometimes he'd be on violin, with me at the piano. They called him Big Brother and me Little Brother.

'It was about this time I remember hearing a band that Bud Scott had touring around. Up in that part of the country they mostly had string bands, and Bud Scott from Natchez had the best band up there. They had fourteen violins – Mark and Forrest Hawkins and Chinaman Walter were three – and Bud himself was playing mandolin. He was a wonderful singer.'

The Forty Fours

Dehlco Robert and Friday, it can be assumed, acquainted Little Brother with a rudimentary piano blues that went under the cryptic title of *The Forty-Fours*. In its basic form – as recalled by Brother – this piece shows a simple arrangement: with the first beat of the measure the bass climbs up to a chordic note, and the right hand follows 'chiming' (chording in the treble) on the other three beats. At this stage it could be mastered by a player without great simultaneous control of both hands.

At Ferriday, the three of them started shaping *The Forty-Fours* into 'the hardest barrelhouse blues of any blues in history to play because you have to keep two different times going in each hand. It's a blues we just steady made up. You could keep adding to it.' When Little Brother Montgomery recorded it nine years later it had grown to an elaborate masterpiece, *Vicksburg Blues*.

The restless life of a juke pianist loosened their prolific alliance. Brother accepted some jobs around Ferriday – at Willards (?), Louisiana for Sam Fillimore, at Clayton, Louisiana, for Fred Douglas, and in Natchez, Mississippi on the other side of the river – landing at St Joseph, Louisiana. 'Then the 1922 high water came and the levee broke at Enoka, Louisiana. There were big floods, and I went to Tallulah.' According to an old resident, the water stood eight feet deep in the streets of Ferriday. Tallulah, Louisiana was not flooded, and Benny Starr engaged Little Brother for his honky-tonk.

'I was there for quite a long time and met Ernest "Flunkey" Johnson, Ragging Willie Wells and Stiff Arm Eddie. All of those were great piano players. And we had Eddie Major and Mancy.' Always keen on extending his pianistic abilities he seized the opportunity to exchange ideas – especially with Flunkey, a cousin of Dehlco Robert. 'Nearly everybody was trying to play *The Forty-Fours*, but Ernest came to be king – King of the Forty-Fours. We called him 44 Flunkey and Ernest 44. Well, the singing came from Black Texas. I used to work with her for Starr. She sang with Ernest too.' Brother accompanied one of her blues with *The Forty-Fours* – eventually the melody became an integral part of his version.

In his Tallulah days, Little Brother made a few excursions – for example, to Monroe and Dehlco, Louisiana. Sondheimer, Louisiana, proved to be an important stop. 'Son Young was there. He was a good ragtime player and inspired me to write *Shreveport Farewell*. I learned *Chinese Man Blues* from him; he got it from Joe Martin. Lee Green was pressing clothes in a place down there, and he'd always come to the juke to learn how to play *The Forty-Fours*. He got them, finally, and taught them to Roosevelt Sykes.'

Eventually Brother left Tallulah for Mound, Louisiana. 'Then I came to Vicksburg, Mississippi, and played for Zach Lewis' nightclub at 1014 Washington Street. I also performed at the Steamboat Exchange, Fitzhugh's, Bell's Café and a lot of places.'

The juke joints of the red-light district gave work to many other pianists. 'Ernest Johnson was playing for Alice on Mulberry Street. In Vicksburg, I ran across Tommy Jackson – he was a great piano player – and Mancy. Son Cook and Johnny Yeager tried to play *The Forty-Fours*, but they weren't any good.

'From Vicksburg I went back to Louisiana, played Transylvania and around, all up through Eudora, Arkansas, and ended up in Arkansas City where I heard Joe Martin at Mama Teddy's nightclub. I picked up his blues, the *Joe Martin Blues*. Skinny Head Pete was in Arkansas too. In Lake Village I met Burnt Face Jake. Them guys were great piano players.'

It seems impossible to lay down a reliable chronology of Brother's movements in the mid-1920s. He travelled extensively in the areas round Louisiana and Mississippi, and the available information is somewhat confusing. He probably bought his first car when he was eighteen years old. Thus he could traverse the country playing 'one-nighters'. In 1923, Little Brother returned home. Still a teenager, he had gathered the experience and reputation of a man.

Gas station in Tchula, Mississippi, 1968.

New Orleans

'There's a vast difference here in this town', said Dominguez of New Orleans. 'Uptown folk all ruffians, cut up in the face and live on the river. All they know is get out on the levee and truck cotton, be longshoremen, screwmen.' Violinist Paul Dominguez was a Creole of Colour. 'You see, we downtown people, we try to be intelligent. Everybody learn a trade. All us people try to get an easy job that our education qualifies us for.' In their simplification these remarks illustrate the social disparity between the two traditional coloured groups in New Orleans, the 'Latin', catholic, bourgeois mulattos in downtown and the 'American', protestant, proletarian Negroes in uptown.

Around the turn of the century, the music of both parts was still rather heterogeneous. Big Eye Louis Nelson started playing clarinet at that time: 'Uptown, in the American part, other side of Canal Street, the people had a different way. They worked in white folks' houses or down along the river. They were more sociable and more like entertainers. They played more rougher, more head music, more blues.' The downtown Creoles played more polite, more conventional sheet music. Guitarist Johnny St Cyr spent his formative years downtown, north-east of Canal

Uptown New Orleans, 1968.

Street: 'The blues I'm sure came from uptown. The uptown bands played the blues, and when in later years they began hiring downtown bands uptown, they started playing blues because that's what they *had* to play.' Like countless others, veteran bassist Pops Foster came from the surrounding country: 'Buddy Bolden's band played a lot of blues. If a band is playing for Negroes and can't play the blues it won't go over.' The strong rural element uptown ensured a constant demand for blues. 'Sometimes we would be playing for a rough bunch that wanted nothing but the blues all night long,' related clarinettist Emile Barnes, once member of blues trumpeter Chris Kelly's band. 'Legitimate' orchestras came under the influence of the rich blues underground in uptown New Orleans. Big Eye Louis Nelson observed that the blues has given jazz more than just a vehicle for improvisation: 'The blues always been. Blues is what cause the fellows to start jazzing.'

Before regular dance bands absorbed the blues, it had been featured by little string groups and pianists. In the first decade of this century, for example, there was an outfit in the uptown Garden District composed of Henry Marcell, guitar; Bob Marcell, mandolin; Bud Roussell, string bass; and Buster Anderson, piano; and all of them were vocalists. Jelly Roll Morton was a Creole, but he worked uptown as well: 'Back in 1901 and 1902, we had a lot of great blues players that didn't know nothing but the blues. Game Kid was the favourite of the Garden District. He was a man that really wouldn't work. Game Kid played the piano all day long after he got up, moving around from one girl's house to another – not for any financial purpose at all, but just to have a good time.' Louis Armstrong as a teenager 'would make the round of the honky-tonks watching the people and laughing at the drunks. We were always looking for a new piano player with something new on the ball, like a rhythm that was all his own. These fellows with real talent often came from the levee camps. They'd sit on a piano stool and beat out some of the damnedest blues you ever heard in your life.'

Not much later, young Louis was playing with a typical barrel-house combination: piano, plus cornet and drums. Johnny St Cyr remembered: 'They were just playing the blues and *Sister Kate*. Then, however, they called it *Who Threw The Bricks On Katy's Head?* Just a few little things they had worked up. Boogus could only play on the black keys of the piano. This was the roughest part of town and Spano's was one of the roughest places down there.' Spano's tonk was situated in the Battlefield, a sort of illegitimate uptown pendant to the downtown Storyville, the only legally constituted red-light district in the United States (1898–1917).

Often very accomplished, the pianists working solo in the brothels were called 'professors'. Some of them had a heavy blues background, and a remarkable number made records: Jelly Roll Morton, Clarence Williams, Buddy Christian, Fred Washington, Arthur Campbell, Steve Lewis, George Thomas, Richard M. Jones, Spencer Williams, Chicken Henry, and Frank Amacker. Pops Foster knew many 'professors': 'They all sat on the bench out there and when there's a little party in one of the rooms a piano player is picked out who goes in and plays all night. That's the way those guys made their money back in those days. When they wanted to play in a band they had to play another instrument. They didn't use piano in a band.' Before the era of hot piano it was looked upon as a 'sissy' instrument, and there was no need for a piano in the standard line-up of cornet, trombone, clarinet, violin, guitar, string bass, and drums. The society orchestras normally had female pianists who could read music. Probably after the closing of Storyville the scene changed – pianos began turning up in jazz bands.

For a 'professor' it was comparatively easy to fit into a larger group; only the less limited tonk players were accepted in jazz orchestras. Most of them never left the barrelhouse arena, but whether strictly blues men or not, they were always welcome at one of the informal private affairs, like the house and lawn parties and the 'fish fries'. Here a beginner could win his spurs, as did Walter Lewis: 'That's the way it started – you just play some night, mostly Saturday night. Somebody gave a supper and he'd hang a red light outside so people would know that's where the supper is at. They used to call it fish fries. When you go there they got a piano, you go in and you play. You got this moonshine whiskey and homebrew. Real old, but to me it was new because I was young. I didn't know, just went along with the crowd.'

On all kinds of occasions these pianists would get together for a 'bucking' contest. Alton Purnell was part of the scene in the late 1920s: 'The piano in New Orleans was all the go, and there were a gob of pianists around in those days. Most every house had a piano in it. New Orleans, you know, is divided into wards, and in every ward they had someone who they thought was their best piano player. One piano player would stop at a house and start playing, and people would come in off the street to listen. Then someone would send for another piano player from a different ward, and then the party might go on for four or five days. The winner was a matter of public opinion.'

Frequently they gathered in a honky-tonk. 'Blues was all I played when I was going there,' emphasised Tuts Washington.

Tuts Washington in front of his house in New Orleans, 1968.

'They'd have me to playing that, and sometimes three or four other piano players would be in the place. We used to buck one another to see who's the best. Me and Brother Montgomery used to meet up in the joints. He was quite young then too – I guess around 1926, '27. Well, he was another one had a good name around here as a good blues playing pianist. I was bumming around with him around Iberville and Marais.'

As a child Little Brother had already been to New Orleans with his family to see some relatives. The city was to become one of his second homes. It is not clear if he got his first footing there before, or after, his Ferriday–Tallulah–Vicksburg period. In any case, he used to live on South Claiborne Street and worked on

Red Cayou in California, early 1940s.

419 Saratoga and at Dodo & Red Bob's barrelhouse on the corner of Calliope and Franklin Street – right in the notorious Battlefield. This area attracted many other pianists, like Pinetop Smith, whom he met in Ponchatoula, Louisiana, about 1923 – probably when Brother was on his way to New Orleans.

The local differences that Paul Dominguez talked about were fading. In Brother's time young Creoles rubbed elbows with the dark uptowners. He moved about in a loose circle with Tuts Washington, Little Willie, Fats Pichon, Red Cayou, Walter Lewis, and Little Dooky. 'Hezekiah was a hell of a good piano player. We had a boy played pretty good called Kid Clayton. He played trumpet and piano. Fact I played with him, and Sam Morgan, when I was seventeen, eighteen years old. Bad Ann Cook used to be around the tonks. She was real bad – killed about six people. As for the blues piano players – they had a lot of them. I heard of Drive 'Em Down. Poree Nolan was an old-timer. Now the greater piano players I always listened to was guys like Udell Wilson and Joe Robichaux. Udell was playing with Lee Collins at the Entertainer's, and Steve Lewis was with Piron. He played kind of on the order of Jelly Roll Morton. They all played ragtime, blues, and jazz. Fate Marable had a band on the boat, the steamer *Capitol*. He was a good pianist.' Little Brother and trumpeter Kid Sheik knew each other for decades, presumably from the early 1920s when Kid Sheik played piano at 'fish fries'. Brother left New Orleans for East Louisiana then, but he often returned to the Crescent City. Probably during one of his visits in the 1930s he met two younger pianists, Little Sammy and the highly gifted Burnell Santiago.

West Florida and Out West

'The bands in New Orleans played jazz', asserted Little Brother, and there is no reason to doubt it – even the rather 'straight' riverboat orchestras sounded hot in those days. He listened to the groups of Buddy Petit, Chris Kelly, Wooden Joe Nicholas, and Kid René, some of the better-known trumpeters. 'There was another band with Tuts Johnson from Baton Rouge on trumpet and Johnny Handy on clarinet.' New Orleans outfits toured on a large scale – mostly along the Gulf Coast, from Florida to Yucatan. All over the country similar orchestras could be found. In one of them Brother got his first band job:

Left to right *Kid Sheik, Little Sammy and George Lewis in Lakeland, Louisiana, probably 1930s.*

'From New Orleans I went to Slidell, Louisiana, and played with Leonard Parker's band. That was a steady organisation.' The personnel, as remembered by Brother and George Lewis, was Leonard Parker, trumpet; Dan Moody, trombone; George Lewis, clarinet; Ralph Laurent, violin; Little Brother Montgomery, piano; probably an unknown player on guitar or banjo; Hosea Harris, string bass and vocal, and possibly Papa Sweet, drums. 'That was about 1924.'

Brother could acquire a new number quickly, and evidently it was not too difficult for him to cope with the somewhat diverse repertoire. Although the blues was the backbone of his music he was versatile enough to fill his role in a band of this size. Not much later he led his own little group in Gulfport, Mississippi, where he lived on 30th Avenue and played at Curtis Coleman's place, 'across the branch'. With him were Trombone Red and a drummer called Ed. 'I played around Biloxi and Pass Christian too, just with a drummer. In Gulfport, I ran across Willie Evans – he was a piano player. I met Willie Parker at Camp Rolling (?), Mississippi, and Percy Miller – he also was in Picayune, Mississippi, and Bogalusa, Louisiana. I played a lot of camps – lumber camps and logging camps. I lived there too and got twenty-five dollars a week, room and board. At a time I was playing in one of those logging camps – I had a drummer with me, and this guy called Harp-Blowing Rabbit come in and blow that harp so people quit gambling. He was working down there – must have been in 1925 or so. And I played in a camp for Tom Payne in Bush, Louisiana – that's below Bogalusa.'

Brother frequently stopped in Bogalusa; blues singer and guitarist Roosevelt Holts saw him there in the mid-1920s. For a while the great Buddy Petit was in town. Pianist Octave Crosby from New Orleans played a job with him: 'Petit wasn't much of a reader but he had a good ear. His band didn't use no music, except for an occasional lead-line for the trumpet player.' About 1925, Brother was in Buddy's band in Bogalusa. Of the other musicians he could only remember Green, reeds; Ralph Laurent, violin; and on string bass, Dan Moody, who had been leading his own dance group there. 'They had a particularly good band in Bogalusa, the Rhythm Aces. I introduced a couple of the guys in the band to the founder of the band, like Willie Esters and Hanson Severe – piano players. Another one who played in Bogalusa at that time was called Charlie Mahorner – he was a great blues player. Sabato Ard and Martin Davis were pretty good piano players. Frenchman Joe was there too.'

The following episode has escaped Brother's memory. Guitarist Ise Youngblood reported: 'I knew Brother Montgomery in Bogalusa and Lumberton and all around. We just stayed together. They called him Brother and me Brother-in-law. Me and him

Above *Ise Youngblood in Tylertown, Mississippi, 1966.*
Right *Walter Lewis in New Orleans, 1960.*

used to play together. That was before he made records. I was quite young then.'

Working with blues guitarists became a habit for Little Brother. 'I didn't meet Big Joe Williams until 1926. We played for Kid Washington in Picayune, Mississippi; Mobile, Alabama, and Electric Mills, Mississippi.' Big Joe threw more light on the kind of job they had: 'I played in lots of sporting houses. The first one I played in was in Electric Mills – me and Little Brother Montgomery. Kid Washington used to go to New Orleans to get musicians to play in the house. He would also go to Birmingham or Texas to get both girls, and musicians, to work. They featured entertainment in the houses – for different people coming to see the girls. While they were making their choice, they'd give them a good show.

FRI. SAT. & SUN.
WALTER LEWIS
IN THE
PIANO BAR
OF THE AIR CONDITIONED AND BEAUTIFUL
COLONIAL CLUB
1306 UPPERLINE

They didn't have no stage or anything. You'd be playing in the hall or just in a room there. The landlady'd bring the girls out in the hall; the guys would be standing around, and you'd play the music, and they'd do their acts. They'd dance and twist around to show off to the guys what they had.'

Little is known about Brother's trips into southern Arkansas and western Louisiana, but it is likely that this line from his *Frisco Hi-Ball Blues* has some autobiographical content: 'Oakdale's on the mountain, Cravens on the Santa Fé, and I'm going to DeRidder and catch the longest train I see.' He probably saw most of the places mentioned in his recollections of other pianists. 'Will Ezell played in Fullerton, Oakdale, DeRidder and DeQuincy – Louisiana. I didn't meet him there – they only told me about him. No Leg Kenny was in Oakdale and DeQuincy too. Charlie Segar is a cousin of mine; he's from Lake Charles. Walter Lewis was in Haynesville, Louisiana; El Doradoh, Arkansas, and Vicksburg, Mississippi. In Tallulah he played for Benny Starr. Also Ruben Walker used to be in Haynesville and ElDorado.' Big Boy Knox was also probably a Louisiana pianist. His playing shows an intriguing similarity to Brother's blues, and Knox's *Blue Man Blues* is the same song as *I Keep On Drinking*, one of the Montgomery standards. Anyway, Little Brother said, 'I lived in Shreveport quite a bit'.

Mississippi

Joe Montgomery at Big Mike's, North Wells St., Chicago, 1966.

In the early 1920s the Montgomery clan moved from Kentwood to Norfield, Mississippi, another sawmill town. Eurreal's younger brothers Joe and Tollie followed in his footsteps although they didn't leave the family in such a sudden way, and his sister Aris had given birth to a son who was to become a much-recorded pianist: Paul Gayten. Norfield is not far from Summit, McComb and Magnolia, the playing ground of Herman Hill, Sudan Washington, and Cooney Vaughn. Shep Hunter, an itinerant pianist from Crystal Springs, Mississippi, remembered the latter two and Little Brother who 'mostly hung around the gambling table'. Brother admittedly liked to play 'cotch', the three-card Spanish poker. One thing he really loved was listening to Cooney Vaughn. 'I thought he was the greatest of anybody at the time, which he was.

'Cooney was from Hattiesburg, Mississippi, and there was another great one from there called Blind Jug – also B. J. Prescott.

Blind Homer was a juke piano player, and Gus Perryman – he was a musicianer, you know, played by notes. Black Emile was from Hattiesburg. We called him Brown Mule – he chewed that brand of tobacco.' Like Bogalusa and Mobile, this town was favoured by touring New Orleans jazz men, and the local pianists often had the chance to join them.

Near Jackson, Brother had a chauffeur who played a little guitar: 'I met Johnnie Temple in 1923, '24. He drove me to Pelahatchie, Mississippi, and around there. He didn't play with me then – just listened. I knew Hainey in D'Lo and Sanatorium. He was a piano player. Monkey Joe and Coot Davis were from D'Lo.' Johnnie Temple recalled that Little Brother lived at D'Lo, Mississippi, for a time and played a barrelhouse circuit from Canton to Morton, Mississippi, and via D'Lo down to Bogalusa. Temple's vocal style and his *New Vicksburg Blues* reflect the impact of Brother's singing.

'I didn't play much in the Delta,' remarked Brother. Sometime during the 1920s he had a job in Greenwood with drummer Buddy Bolden from New Orleans. 'Our train stopped in Durant, Mississippi, and this old Papa Charlie Jackson was on the same train. He was going to Greenwood too. I met Tommy Jackson in Rosedale; he used to live there. In Greenville I ran across Freddie Coates – great piano player. He was playing in the Delta, like Milas Davis and Asthma Slim – that's Piano Slim. I didn't meet Friday Ford until 1923.'

Blues singer and guitarist Skip James claimed to have teamed up with Brother in Yazoo City, Mississippi, to go to Vicksburg, but Brother does not remember Skip. In any case, James's *Special Rider Blues* is derived from Montgomery's *No Special Rider Blues*. 'When I was a little boy in Mississippi, I used to run around and follow the bands through the streets,' said Willie Dixon, who was born in Vicksburg in 1915. 'They had the band up on the back of a truck and I loved it. I remember Little Brother up on the truck playing piano. You've got to hear him do *Farish Street Jive*. It's the most beautiful thing. Years ago they called it Dudlow.' Little Brother's commentary upon hearing Lee Green's *Dud-Low Joe* was: 'He's trying to play *Farish Street Jive*.'

'In Vicksburg, I met a guy who was looking for a piano player. He came from Canton, so I went over there to play for him. That's where I met Sunnyland Slim the first time. From then on I played for several guys who ran places in Canton – Tom Payne, Will Hay, Sam Williams – tonks, you know. I also played in a band

Above *Sunnyland Slim.*
Right *Danny Barker in front of the New Orleans Jazz (Club) Museum, Dumaine St., New Orleans, 1968.*

in Canton – Eugene Watts' Serenaders. We travelled too, played dance halls.' The Serenaders consisted of Allen Snodgrass, trumpet; Eugene Watts, trombone; Green, saxophone; Little Brother Montgomery, piano; Frank Johnson, banjo, and Odie Berry, drums.

In the summer of 1927, Brother was back in New Orleans. The Alley Cabaret on North Claiborne and St Bernard streets enjoyed a good reputation among both musicians and gamblers. 'I was considered too young to hang around a place of this kind but the manager, Octave Clements, knew my folks and if I had my banjo he would let me in,' told Danny Barker. 'When the regular banjo player, Wellington Dolton, saw me he would call me, give me money, cigarettes and drinks so that I would play in his place as he ran to the gambling table or somewhere. There was a very good jazz band playing there. Maurice Durand on cornet; Big Eye Louis Nelson, clarinet; Odette Davis, piano; George Henderson, drums, and Nelishi Briscoe sang and entertained.

'One night I went to the Alley early. The band had not yet arrived. I heard the piano playing in the cabaret and what I heard excited me because I'd never heard a blues played so slowly, so sad and so complicated before. I was puzzled because I had thought that I could play all tempos. What I was hearing on the piano that night was a tempo which was precise – on time, in time, but slower than a funeral march. I entered the cabaret in the rear and went up to the piano.

'The man was playing for his own pleasure and smiling with his eyes closed. He was softly singing to himself. He played on and on and finally, looking around at me he said nicely, "You like these blues?" "I sure do – what's the name of them blues?" "This is the *Vicksburg Blues*." He played. I listened. After he had finished I asked him his name. "Little Brother." "You from in town?" "No, I'm from Kentwood, Louisiana. I'll be in town until Friday and then I'm going to Mississippi for a few weeks and hustle some money and then I'm coming back here."

'He asked if I was a musician and I said, "I got a banjo. I'm learning." "Get your box out. Listen – when I play slow you play the first chord on the beat and then tremolo the rest of the bar." He played an introduction and told me the key and then I played like he had told me to. "That's it, you catch on quick." We played on and on. I noticed that a crowd from the gambling room had gathered and stood around listening. We both looked around when we heard a trumpet playing real beautiful. It was Guy Kelly, the great trumpet player from Baton Rouge. While we kept playing Guy walked slowly up till he reached the stand. It was a thrill to me, playing with Guy and Little Brother. We continued to play until the band arrived. The drummer and Big Eye Louis joined the session. Dolton was happy – he was free to go to the gambling table. Guy was off that night and we played all night long.'

Brother persuaded Danny's mother to let her son make the trip through Mississippi in Brother's Ford. 'We talked as we rode the dusty brown gravel roads and passed the small towns and villages. Little Brother was a master at travelling through the South. I noticed that he never stopped at any place that was owned or operated by white folks. When he wanted to stop for food or drink he would ask some coloured person where there was a coloured place. He drove slowly and carefully when passing through a community. He watched the road like a hawk, but when we hit the outskirts he'd sigh and relax.

'At about six that evening we arrived in Crystal Springs, Mississippi, and drove across the railroad tracks down a hill to a settlement of coloured people. When we pulled up in front of a café the men standing in front of the place looked curiously at the little Ford. When Little Brother stepped out they smiled and greeted him. He was well known there. He shook hands with each of them and called me over to introduce me. We entered the café and met the owner, after which we sat down to a fine meal of fried chicken and cat head biscuits. The owner and Little Brother laughed and talked; they planned a juke dance that night, to be held in the rear of the café. All that was necessary to hold one of these dances in a hurry was to send a couple of men and boys from house to house to inform the populace that some music men were in town and there'd be a juker that night. When we started to play the large back room was really full of folks who were all wide-eyed and smiling. After a couple of dances, the sheriff walked in, followed by two coloured men who carried gallon jugs of "smoke" – that's what they called that moonshine whiskey. They brought in about twenty gallons of smoke and placed them under a long table. Then the folks started drinking. We played and played and the place really jumped. The sheriff took a seat near the door and watched us as we played. I kept my eye on him as he took off his two large ugly-looking pistols and placed them on the table. The waiters served him a large platter of fried chicken and cat heads.'

Nothing serious happened, and they continued playing juke dances in towns like Pineville, Brookhaven and Vicksburg. 'We drove on to Summit, Mississippi, and there located a piano player named Herman Hill. He and Little Brother were very happy to see one another and we went to Herman's house where his wife treated us like relatives. She washed our soiled clothing and cooked up a lot of fine food. Herman Hill had an old upright piano in his front room and he and Brother played and talked about dozens of other pianists they knew, how they played and their songs and what towns they were in. Little Brother and Herman Hill took turns playing all the evening and night. Neighbours and friends came by and stayed to listen and enjoy this music. They played music I'd never heard before. All kinds of blues and original piano solos. As they played they discussed the lyrics and the different meanings of moods, and they talked of how other pianists had interpreted these same songs.

'When we were safely back in New Orleans my mother was so happy to see me; she sat us down at the table to eat some wonderful gumbo. "How was the trip?" she asked us. "Did you all have any trouble?" We both gave her the same reply: "Not a thing happened." I had nearly two hundred dollars which I showed mother. "Mississippi ain't so bad after all," was her remark.'

Brother didn't stay long. In Norfield he picked up drummer Henry Ross and went to Jackson, Mississippi. 'Together we got forty dollars a night. In Jackson, I played at the Red Circle Hall, the Morrison Hall, the Crystal Palace and at the Red Castle for Ed Garrett. Brick Roseby fooled around with us on sax – at house

Crystal Palace Recreational Center, North Farish St., Jackson, Mississippi, 1958.

parties. They had some other piano players there – Little Low Friday, Charley Taylor, Monkey Joe. The first time I met Coot Davis was in Jackson. Tommy Johnson lived there in Doodaville – was around Vicksburg too. He played mandoline and could do more than anybody else on the guitar. I was playing over in East Jackson for Ellis Reynolds when Clarence Desdune came with his band.'

Desdune

Clarence Desdune's Joyland Revelers, once known as Piron Number Two, were organised in New Orleans. Desdune was a qualified violinist, and the musicians he chose had to be sight-readers. Early in 1928, the orchestra was playing at the Pythian Temple Roof Garden, probably with George McCullum, trumpet; Raymond Brown, trombone; Earl Fouché, Felix Goff, Harold Dejan, reeds; Harry Fairconnetue, banjo; Pops Kimball, bass; and Shine Williams, drums. When Fouché and Goff left, saxophonist Edgard Saucier and pianist Warren Bennett came in for a while before the band went on a six-month tour through the Midwestern states.

Jackson was the first city on their way. They were looking for the best pianist in town willing to join the Joyland Revelers – and they found Little Brother. On their first job – in Yazoo City – the band consisted of George McCullum, trumpet; Raymond Brown, trombone; Harold Dejan, Oliver Alcorn, Lucien Johnson, reeds; Clarence Desdune, violin and banjo; Little Brother Montgomery, piano; Harry Fairconnetue, banjo; Pops Kimball, bass; and Shine Williams, drums.

Desdune's orchestra used stock orchestrations, most of them written by Archie Bleyer and Frank Skinner; they had a book of Ted Lewis arrangements as they normally had a white audience. The jazz standards, however, were played 'by head'. Without the help of Oliver Alcorn, Brother would have been lost in an ocean of sheet music. Each time a new number arrived Oliver would study it with him so that he could 'fake' his part the following night. Now and again he broke up the routine: Harold Dejan reported that Little Brother stopped a dance in St Joseph, Missouri, 'with his great piano playing and blues singing. He had one blues that would catch the attention of the dancers, and they'd walk over to the piano to hear him.'

Desdune was very business-minded. He was his own booking agent and only played with his band in a profitable area. Even then, 'he was more off the stand than playing', said Judge Riley who replaced Shine Williams in about 1930. 'Desdune used to control the tickets and count the house. Therefore we had to play a polonaise – made it easier for him to count them. Harry Fairconnetue managed the Joyland Revelers. Unlike Desdune, he was a very good banjo player, according to Harold Dejan. 'Sometimes Harry would fool Desdune by dropping out at breaks he would usually play, so that Desdune had to take an unexpected solo. We had only two brass in the band – George McCullum and Raymond Brown, but the two sounded like a full section. They

Left *Clarence Desdune's Joyland Revelers:* (left to right) *Harry Fairconnetue, Harold Dejan, George McCullum, Shine Williams and Raymond Brown, 1928.*
Right *Oliver Alcorn on the boat (with Sidney Desvigne?), late 1930s.*

were bosom buddies – we called them Little Gut and Big Gut. George left when his wife had a baby, and he was replaced by Alvin Alcorn. I guess Alvin joined in Wayne, Nebraska. We all made plenty of money until we came to Desdune's home town, Omaha. His father's band was very popular there, and for some reason the people didn't take to the son as to the father. Little Brother left us in Omaha.'

Chicago

Above *The Owl Theater on 47th St. and State St., Chicago, 1968.*

Right *Sweet Williams, Chicago, 1968.*

'I quit the Joyland Revelers in Omaha, Nebraska, which was our headquarters, and come to Chicago the last of 1928', recalled Brother. 'At that time they had mostly jazz around. I met quite a few piano players, like Earl Hines, Teddy Wilson, Henry Palmer, Bob Alexander, Zinky Cohn, Jerome Carrington, and Leo Montgomery – that's Bob Montgomery's uncle. Clarence Jones was playing at the Owl Theater on 47th and State. Jelly Roll Morton played there too – he always carried a .38 Special to protect his thousand-dollar bill. Jelly Roll, Fats Waller and Old Man Clarence Jones used to hang around Dickerson's music shop, run by Aletha Dickerson and her husband, Bob Alexander. He gave me the first piano lessons in my life.'

Like uptown New Orleans, Chicago had its share of the rural Deep South, with Southern habits and Southern music. 'Many people out on the South Side held parties to help pay that high rent – house rent parties, they were called', related New Orleans trumpeter Lee Collins. 'Every place that would have these parties was furnished with some kind of piano. House rent party piano

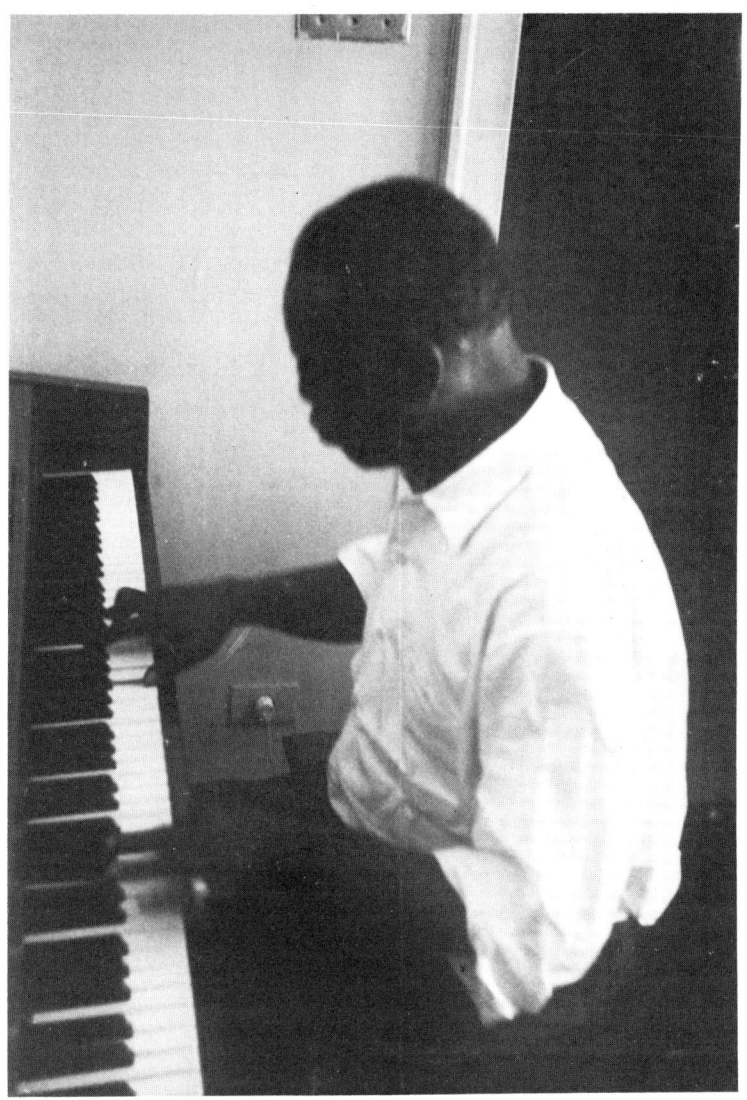

players, or anyone else that could play the blues, would get paid for playing and also would get all the liquor he could drink.'

For a barrelhouse man there was no job in one of the high-bred orchestras in Chicago. Most of the pianists in the large pit-bands had a classical training. Apparently Little Brother worked for himself. 'I played house rent parties practically every night in the

Sweet Williams in Chicago, 1968.

week for different people, such as Robert McGhee, 4048 Indiana, and Malcolm and Weedy Jones, 5758 South State, and around at the Grand Hotel on 31st and State. We played mostly blues and boogies. You wouldn't get a job if you couldn't play the *Chicago Fives*. I met Cow Cow Davenport at the old Angelus Building on 35th and Wabash. We had a guy here played a lot of house parties named Forty-Five. Other good blues players were Jimmy Yancey, Albert Ammons, Meade Lux Lewis, Chicago Bill, Cripple Clarence Lofton and Sweet Williams, and we had Jackie Cuga and Sneed. Blind Blake was there, only he was a guitarist. Toothpick was a house rent player. Hersal Thomas used to run with me and Charlie Spand; we played together for Mrs Booker Lumpkin, 5009 Vincennes. Hersal lived mostly in Detroit, like his brother George Thomas who was more of a writer. Down south I'd hear about Will Ezell and Milas Davis and Ruben Walker, but I met them first in about 1930 – in Chicago. Bob Call followed Ezell. I knew Pinetop Smith here before he got killed on Clark Street. Arnold Wiley and I were going with two sisters, and Irene Wiley, his sister, was married to Doc Parmley, the great trumpet player.'

In the late 1920s, the Chicago based record companies were availing themselves of the potential of unsophisticated blues and boogies, and the talent-scouts did not overlook Little Brother. Art Laibley engaged him for several Paramount recordings in Grafton, Wisconsin, as a soloist and as an accompanist for Irene Scruggs and Minnie Hicks. 'Minnie was a housewife, but Irene – I used to work with her on the TOBA circuit at that time. At the Grand Theater, 31st and State, I played a couple of times with her, and also with Ma Rainey. After I returned from Grafton I played at the King Tut, 47th and Michigan. Professor Cook was the Master of Ceremonies.' Sometimes around this period, or possibly earlier, he made the acquaintance of Eddie Heywood, who was leading the band of the Butterbeans and Susie show.

The Brunswick-Balke-Collender company recorded Minnie Hicks and Little Brother again in January 1931. 'J. Mayo Williams was the agent for the company. So we made records at the Furniture Mart Building, 666 Lake Shore Drive. On *Louisiana Blues* Minnie's husband is playing guitar.' The Depression shook Chicago and caused a decentralisation of the music business. Little Brother returned south where he knew his way around. 'I went back to New Orleans, Louisiana, and stayed down there quite a bit. Then I came to Jackson, Mississippi, and organised my own band. I kept it from around 1931 to '38 or '39.'

Above *American Furniture Mart building, North Lake Shore Drive, Chicago, 1968.*
Left *J. Mayo Williams, South Drexel Ave., Chicago, 1968.*

Southland Troubadours

'The first time I met Little Brother here in Jackson he had six pieces', remembered Butch Roseby, riverboat trombonist and rhythm and blues drummer. 'There was Doc and Luke Parmley, Curly and a drummer from New Orleans – Henry was his name.' This was the nucleus of the Southland Troubadours: Doc Parmley, trumpet; Rosser Emerson, Lucien Johnson, saxophones; Little Brother Montgomery, piano and leader; Curly Guesnon, banjo; Luke Parmley, brass bass; and Henry Ross, drums.

Henry was Brother's 'old side-kick' and the Parmleys 'came from Holtkamp's Georgia Smart Set when the show went bum. I sent for Lucien and Curly.' Guesnon had played with the Sam Morgan band: 'So after Sam suffered his stroke, I joined Lu Johnson's Californians out of Monroe, Louisiana, but after a while this band broke up too. Then I went to Jackson, Mississippi, to play with Little Brother Montgomery and his Southland Troubadours.' Rosser Emerson was perhaps the first, but not the last, musician Brother recruited from the local outfit of minstrel drummer Joe White. When Lucien Johnson left he was replaced by Brick Roseby.

'It was during intermission on a cool April night in 1932,' wrote trumpeter Howard Loach, 'while playing an engagement at the Crystal Palace Ballroom in Jackson with a band headed by Hyram Nichols, when I became personally acquainted with Little Brother, a most talented pianist, who led a seven-piece jazz combo, the Southland Troubadours. That night Little Brother persuaded me to join his band, explaining his contract with a school in the southern part of the state, for that summer. He needed me in order to fulfil his contract which called for eight musicians.

'We spent the entire summer travelling throughout the states of Illinois, Wisconsin, and portions of Michigan, playing engagements by night in the towns where the school's baseball team played against respective local competition during the day. We played ballrooms filled to capacity for the entire summer. There was Doc Parmley, an outstanding trumpet player, who played a style all his own; Rosser Emerson, equally as talented on alto saxophone; Brick Roseby, a stylist in his own right, playing alto sax too. Luke Parmley, Doc's brother, played the tuba; H. T. Hennington on banjo; Henry Ross, a gifted drummer; and there I was holding down second trumpet, and of course, Little Brother,

Butch Roseby in front of his house, Banks St., Jackson, Mississippi, 1968.

pianist and leader.' The same personnel is given in the Chicago *Defender* of 11 June 1932; the note mentions a tour of Minnesota, Wisconsin, Iowa, and Illinois by Little Brother Montgomery and his Southland Troubadour band from Jackson, Mississippi.

The Collegiate Orchestra: (standing, left to right) *H. T. Hennington, Henry Ross, Brick Roseby, Doc Parmley, Luke Parmley;* (seated, left to right) *Howard Loach, Little Brother Montgomery, Rosser Emerson, Washington Island, Wisconsin, 1932.*

Howard Loach continued, 'That enjoyable summer ended much too soon and we returned to Jackson and resumed the name of the Southland Troubadours after travelling under the name of the Collegiate Ramblers, which was more befitting while under contract with the school. This was my first full-time employment as a musician with full-time pay. Playing with a well-organised band was most alluring to me. I enjoyed it immensely and learned a lot working with an experienced group.

'It was then that Little Brother decided to augment the band to ten pieces. That's when I met Curly Guesnon, previously a member of the Southland Troubadours, who replaced the present banjoist. Louis Charles, trombone, and Doug Blackmon, sax, were added. We then took to the road playing one-night engagements on a percentage basis. J. C. Woodard, accordion, played with the band on numerous occasions as a special attraction but was not a full-fledged member during my tour of duty. I remained with the band until September 1933, when I left for Chicago.'

Talking about the band's music Curly Guesnon declared that 'what they played wasn't New Orleans; it was mostly stock, like *Mule Face Blues*. Doc Parmley wouldn't know a note as big as a house, and they was playing all those stocks and tricky numbers, all that staccato, he'd be right up there with the rest of the brass, making it note for note. As long as Doc didn't hear Loach play a new number he couldn't make it. Loach was a master musician; he helped me to become an excellent reader.' Jesse Steele, saxophone, and probably Man Henderson, trumpet, joined the band after the departure of Howard Loach. Brother recalled having led a ten-piece orchestra in Jackson at the Red Castle on Bailey Avenue – presumably the Southland Troubadours after 1932.

'We got some offers to record, but we didn't care because we had good jobs', said Luke Parmley. 'We often played on the radio. When we come into a town we'd broadcast for half an hour to stir up the folks. Then we gave a concert in the evening and played for dancing at night. We travelled all around.' Little Brother recounted some of the orchestras working in the same territory: 'Sidney Desvigne out of New Orleans, C. S. Belton out of Florida, George E. Lee out of Kansas City, Papa Celestin out of New Orleans, Mark Hawkins out of Natchez, Mississippi, Harry Walker out of Monroe, Louisiana. We broadcasted over WCOC in Meridian, Mississippi, Rosser Emerson's home town. Nat Towles had a band in Omaha, but he joined us for a while when his band broke up.'

By 1937, Henry Ross had left Little Brother for Jeter-Pillars Club Plantation Orchestra in St Louis. Little Brother and Curly alternated with the band of Joe White, which featured the young Louis Jordan. In the years following 1934, the Southland Troubadours were a rather unstable organisation, and finally they fell apart in the late 1940s. Luke was their booking agent: 'We had Duke Huddleston and Lucius Stokes on sax. For a season some of us went with George Naylor; he had a Georgia minstrel show. Tommy Jackson helped out on piano when Little Brother was away.'

Despite his swing-band activities Brother never lost touch with

Joe White's band: (left to right) *Butch Roseby, unknown, Ed Roseby, unknown, Joe White, 2 unknowns, probably J. C. Woodard, probably Gene Porter, Rosser Emerson, Jackson, Mississippi, c. 1931.*

the Jackson blues scene. Tompy was his drummer for house rent parties after Henry Ross had left. Monkey Joe was there, and his half-brother Coot Davis, Harry Carter and, now and then, Cooney Vaughn. In these surroundings, Otis Spann and his cousin Johnny Jones developed their talent as blues pianists. 'Me and my brother Joe taught Otis how to play when he was nine or ten years old,' stated Brother. Spann's *S.P. Blues* is a version of *The Forty-Fours*, and Monkey Joe's *New York Central* is nothing else but Little Brother's *Vicksburg Blues* with different lyrics.

In summer 1935, Brother, Monkey Joe, Harry Carter, and guitarist Walter Jacobs journeyed to New Orleans to cut some records for RCA-Victor. A year later, Little Brother returned with his old friend Ernest 44, Ernest's vocalist Tommy Griffin, Walter Jacobs, the Carter brothers – Bo, Lonnie, and Sam, and four other blues artists Bo Carter seems to have located in the

Delta. Curly Guesnon recalled the incident: 'One day Little Brother came to New Orleans and paid me a visit. He had a recording session at the St Charles Hotel and asked me to come along. So when we got there, he starts making a few numbers and during the break I say, "Brother, I got a little number I wrote, *Goodbye, Good Luck To You*. You want to play it with me?" He agrees and sits down to play while I sing. Somebody in the studio hears it and offers me ten dollars if I want to record the number. I didn't know nothing about recording and I was broke, so I sang the number and this was the first time I made a record.' This session also marked the debut of singer Annie Turner, a fifteen-year-old native of the Crescent City. No alternate takes were made, and so supervisor Eli Oberstein managed to produce thirty-seven sides on a single day. Little Brother's output of twenty-three numbers demonstrates his remarkable musicianship. Regarding his known recordings, he made a puzzling statement: 'I made records for Bluebird way before August 10, 1935 – I was recording for them in 1933.'

From time to time Brother resumed his life as juke player and disappeared into the backwoods. In the late 1930s, K. C. Douglas heard him in a logging camp for the Pearl Valley Lumber Company at Carthage, Mississippi. Little Brother himself knew another barrelhouse pianist in this region: 'Box Car played for Sam White – in Philadelphia and Carthage, and he was in Fannin, Mississippi. He got his name because he slept in box cars. 'I left the Southland Troubadours for good in 1939.'

Doc Parmley took over the leadership of the Troubadours from Brother and replaced him with H. T. Hennington, and later, Stuff Pate and Paul Gayten. In August 1940, *Down Beat* magazine reported Little Brother's presence in Yazoo City. His best-liked pieces were *Delta Blues*, *Highway 61* and *Little Brother's Got The Blues*. The *Down Beat* of 15 November 1940 has an article on him (which has proved impossible to find).

'I had an old lady in Texas so I went to Beaumont and stayed awhile, playing gigs. David Lee Johnson was a good piano player around Beaumont, and Peg Top was great. I met Ivory Joe Hunter in Port Arthur, Texas. Then I left and came back to Canton, Mississippi, where my mother and father were then living – they came with a logging outfit – and I played at the Beer Garden in South Canton. I was at the Swing Club in Hattiesburg when World War II came, and I went back to Chicago. I been there ever since.'

Post-War Appendix

Little Brother probably hit Memphis on his way up north – presumably not for the first time as he has a surprising knowledge of the local piano scene, although he was not apparently part of it. Chicago witnessed a second blossoming of 'old-time' jazz, and Brother soon joined the proceedings. He played with most of the New Orleans men still, or again, active – among them Lonnie Johnson, Baby Dodds, John Lindsay, Oliver Alcorn, Ransom Knowling, Nattie Dominique, Bill Johnson, Tony Parenti, Tubby Hall, Preston Jackson, Al Wynn, Porkchop Smith, Edgard Saucier, and Pops Foster. In 1948, the Kid Ory band gave a Carnegie Hall concert with Lee Collins, trumpet; Kid Ory, trombone; Joe Darensbourg, clarinet; Little Brother Montgomery, piano; Bud Scott, guitar; Ed Garland, string bass, and Minor Hall, drums. Brother displayed an amazing capacity for fitting into diverse groups. He became a sort of 'grand old man' of rhythm and blues piano. With both of his hands he tightened the sound in the bands of Sonny Boy Williamson, Otis Rush, and Magic Sam. And he can hold his own in a request spot. 'I think Little Brother can play a thousand numbers.'

Odie Payne may be right.

Little Brother Montgomery and his group: (left to right) *Bob Skiver,* Earl Murphy,* Booker T. Washington, Montgomery, Chicago, early 1960s.*
* or vice versa.

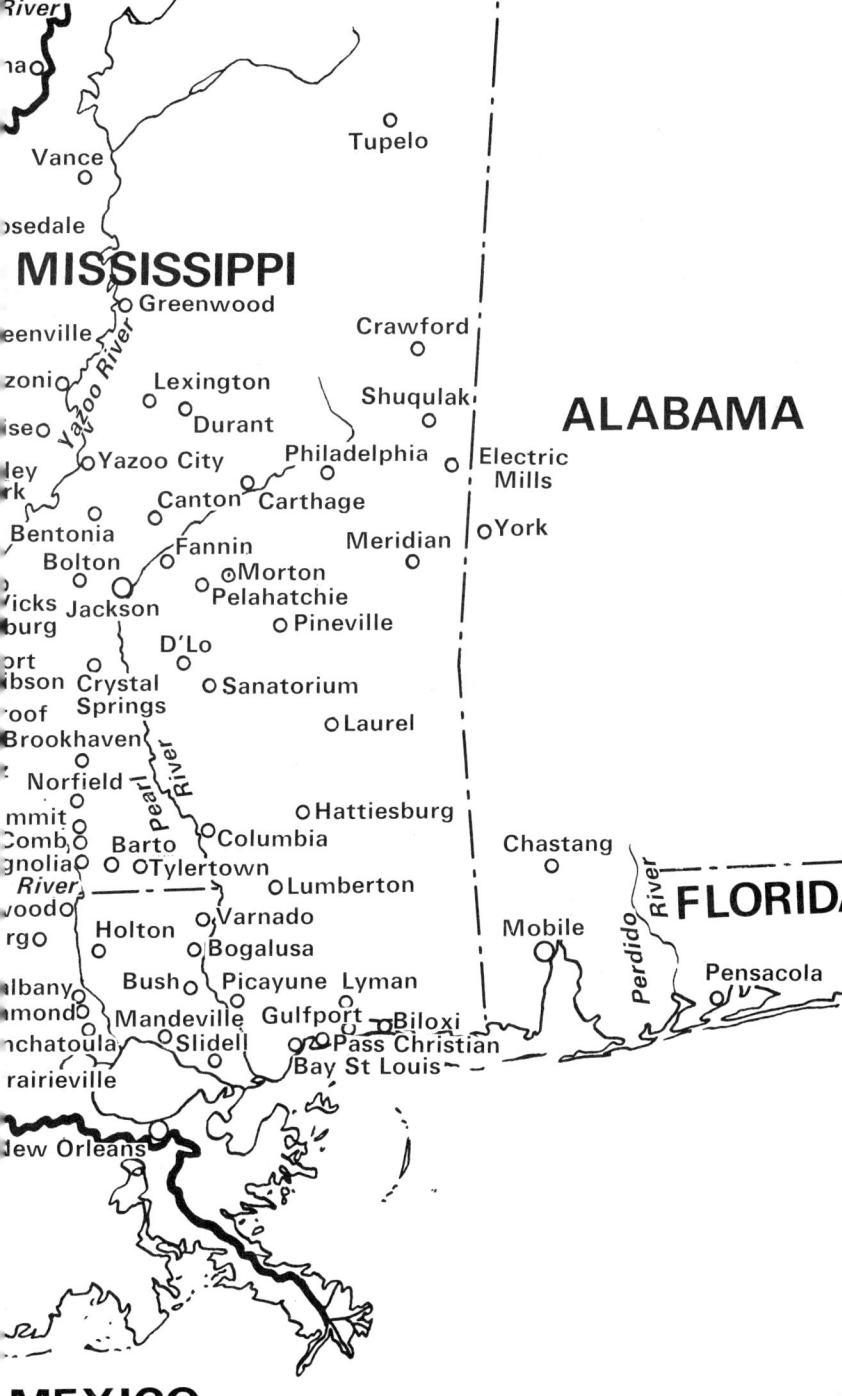

Who's Who

This section gives some data on a number of the musicians turning up in Little Brother Montgomery's life story until 1942. The artists are listed in alphabetical order, under their correct names if known. Cross-references are to be found in the Index.

ALVIN ELMORE 'MICKEY' ALCORN (trumpet) born New Orleans, La., 7 September 1912. Taught by George McCullum and brother Oliver, probably influenced by Buddy Petit. Had own youngsters' band, played jitney dances with Joe Robichaux (piano). Then mostly travelling with reading bands. First recordings with Don Albert and his Orchestra (San Antonio, 1936). After World War II, was in New Orleans groups. Still active in New Orleans in 1970.

OLIVER E. ALCORN (clarinet, alto and tenor saxophone) born New Orleans, La., 3 August 1910. Brother of Alvin, somehow related to George McCullum in whose band he started. Then at the Alley Cabaret with leader Maurice Durand (trumpet), Walter Decou (piano), Wellington Dolton (banjo), and George Henderson (drums). Replaced Polo Barnes in and recorded with Celestin's Original Tuxedo Orchestra (New Orleans, autumn 1927). Rejoined Celestin in the early 1930s, later with Sidney Desvigne on the steamer *Capitol*, and Floyd Campbell. After World War II in Chicago, where he recorded with Little Brother Montgomery (1947) and St Louis Jimmy (1948). Still alive in 1970.

ALBERT AMMONS (piano) born Chicago, Ill., 1907; died 5 December 1949. Father of Gene Ammons (tenor saxophone). Influenced by Hersal Thomas, associated with Meade Lux Lewis, Jimmy Yancey, and Pinetop Smith. Learned boogie at house rent parties; became versatile pianist working with small jazz groups. First recordings in Chicago, 1936. Popularised boogie in the company of Lewis and Pete Johnson from Kansas City. Outstanding player.

VARNADO ANDERSON (piano) born possibly La. Probably a barrel-house player from the east corner of Louisiana. Varnado is a common surname in Tangipahoa Parish, and there is a town named Varnado, 40 miles east of Kentwood.

DANIEL (DANNY) BARKER (guitar, banjo, vocal) born New Orleans, La., 13 January 1909. Well known jazz musician, married to singer Blue Lu Barker. After playing in several local groups, went to New York to play in swing bands. First recordings with Dave Nelson's Harlem Hot Shots (New York, 1931). During the mid-1940s, much sought after New Orleans rhythm man mainly with Pops Foster (string bass) and Baby Dodds (drums). Recorded extensively. Still active in New Orleans in 1970.

Oliver Alcorn, Chicago, 1968.

DOUGLAS (DOUG) BLACKMON (saxophones). In 1929–30, led a band headquartered in El Dorado, Ark., the Kansas City Rhythm Kings, with Doc and Luke Parmley. Played with Joe White, according to Luke.

ARTHUR 'BLIND' BLAKE (guitar, vocal) born probably Fla. or Ga.; probably died *c.* 1940. Excellent solo instrumentalist with unusual band discipline which enabled him to fit into small jazz groups. Probably influenced Big Bill Broonzy; associated with Charlie Spand in Chicago and Detroit in the late 1920s and early 1930s. Travelled extensively despite his blindness.

BOX CAR (piano) born possibly Miss.; died Chicago, Ill., *c.* 1940. Was from Laurel (Little Brother Montgomery) or Port Gibson (Big Joe Williams). Played in Baton Rouge, Slidell, La. (Big Joe) and around Jackson, Miss. (Brick Roseby). Recorded, according to Big Joe.

RAYMOND (RAY) 'BIG GUT' BROWN (trombone, possibly violin) born possibly LaPlace, La., possibly *c.* 1884; died *c.* 1940. Father of Ray Brown (trumpet), father-in-law of H. E. Minor (banjo). Possibly the same person as Raymond Brown, the violinist of Kid Ory's Woodland Band (LaPlace, 1905). Presumably went to New Orleans with Ory. Played trombone with Fats Pichon (1927), Handy's Louisiana Shakers (early 1930s) and Sidney Desvigne.

BOB CALL (piano). Blues man in Chicago, possibly influenced by Cow Cow Davenport. Recorded there in the late 1920s and after World War II. Still living in Chicago in 1968.

HARRY CARTER (CHATMON) (piano, violin, vocal) born probably Bolton, Miss. Member of the large Chatmon clan. Brother Sam Chatmon: 'We started out from our parents – it's just a gift we had in the family. Three or four of us took a few music lessons, but the rest of us grew with it just by ear.' They mostly played in Central Mississippi and the Delta; some of them became known as the Mississippi Sheiks. Harry was still living near Jackson, Miss., in 1960.

JEROME CARRINGTON (piano, alto saxophone, vocal). Trained musician from Baltimore, Md. Mostly working as 'pitman' in Chicago theatre orchestras, e.g. with Doc Cook (1926–7), Erskine

Tate (1927, 1930–3) and Dave Peyton (1929). While with Cook, played at The Nest (name changed to Apex Club) in a trio with Jimmie Noone (clarinet) and Zutty Singleton (drums). Recorded with Half Pint Jaxon (Chicago, 1933), Washboard Rhythm Kings (Camden, N.J., 1936) and probably Cook and His Dreamland Orchestra (Chicago, December 1926). Still living and playing in Washington, D.C., in 1965.

JOSEPH LOUIS 'RED' CAYOU (piano) born New Orleans, La., 4 August 1905; died Oakland, Cal., 7 September 1947. Half-brother of pianists Manuel and Jean Vigne and Cooney Guidry. Cooney and Red started very young, probably inspired by Jean and Jelly Roll Morton who often came to their house. Red played at the Big 25 in a trio with Lorenzo Tio (clarinet) and Caffrey Darensbourg (banjo), but mostly solo in tonks and private houses. Tuts Washington said: 'He was the best thing they had here. He used to play *High Society*, *Twelfth Street Rag* and all them kind of things, all the latest numbers. He was just an all-round fellow. He was a good blues man too. I caught *Mr Freddie Blues* from Red – he heard it on these electric pianos.' Red went to Northern California in the late 1920s, working there solo, and in New Orleans bands. Well remembered and highly respected in New Orleans.

JAMES (JIMMY) 'KID' CLAYTON (trumpet, piano, vocal) born Jasper County, Miss., 2 March 1902; died New Orleans, La., 17 December 1963. Came to New Orleans as a child. Uptown blues specialist, started as 'fish fries' pianist. In the early 1920s, was in Jack Carey's band which 'played the rattiest jazz in New Orleans'. Toured with Dan Moody. Had own band with Tink Baptiste (piano) and Curly Guesnon (banjo) in the late 1920s. Continued to play rough jazz in various New Orleans outfits. Made some recordings on trumpet after World War II.

FREDDIE COATES (piano) born possibly Miss. Delta pianist with a mature blues style. Recorded in 1927, accompanying blues singers Sadie James (Memphis) and Alice Pearson (Chicago). Pearson's *Greenville Levee Blues*, although modelled on Bessie Smith's *Back Water Blues*, reflects own experience, the flooding of Greenville, Miss., in spring 1927. Coates and Pearson were still a team there in the 1930s.

GEORGE 'KID SHEIK' COLAR (trumpet, piano, vocal) born New Orleans, La., 15 September 1908. Started playing blues piano c. 1920, took up trumpet inspired by Wooden Joe Nicholas and Chris Kelly for whom he sat in from time to time. Played second trumpet with Buddy Petit. Marched with Kid René's band (1930s) and the Eureka Brass Band (since 1952). Still blowing strong in New Orleans in 1970. His *Gin Mill Blues* is a nice 'fish fries' boogie.

JESSE 'MONKEY JOE' COLEMAN (piano, vocal) born probably Miss., before 1906. Half-brother of Coot Davis, from D'Lo, Miss. Also played trumpet, trombone, and drums, cracked jokes and tap-danced, according to Johnnie Temple. Worked in jukes around Jackson, Miss. in the early 1930s. Seen in New Orleans by Lemon Nash. Made his first recordings there in 1935, probably recommended by Little Brother Montgomery. Went to Chicago and recorded there in the late 1930s and in 1961 (with Walter Jacobs). Probably still living in Chicago in 1970. His crisp boogie playing was admired by Otis Spann.

'BAD' ANN COOK (vocal) born Franzenville, La., c. 1888; died New Orleans, La., 29 September 1962. Notorious woman of the Battlefield. Her recordings with members of Louis Dumaine's Jazzola Eight prove the existence of a vocal style in New Orleans more 'lowdown' than the 'Creole blues' of Esther Bigeou, Lizzie Miles, and Edna Hicks. Earl Humphrey (trombone) took part in the session (New Orleans, 1927): 'We did ours first and then we went to work on Ann Cook,' who, by the way, had to be pulled out of a bar. 'She was just one of them real outstanding barrelhouse blues singers. You know, sang around home, but she hadn't never sang with a band, sang with piano players. They'd cut in anywhere, they can follow you better than a whole band. Well, she'd cut off some of the bars, just things like that.' Ann Cook became religious and recorded a gospel song accompanied by Wooden Joe's New Orleans Band (New Orleans, 1949).

CHARLES (CHARLIE) 'COW COW' DAVENPORT (piano, vocal) born Anniston, Ala., 23 April 1894; died Cleveland, Ohio, 2 December 1955. As a youngster, played ragtime and blues for private affairs, in honky-tonks and brothels around Birmingham, Ala., playing ground for much piano talent: Pinetop Smith, Jabo Williams, Walter Roland, Arthur Bascomb, Avery Parrish, George Tremer,

Robert McCoy, Mack Rhinehart, Fred Longshaw, even Jelly Roll Morton. Travelled with tent shows, later on the TOBA (Theatre Owners Booking Association) circuit. Frequented Chicago and Detroit in the late 1920s. Settled in Cleveland in the late 1930s. Cut numerous gramophone records and some piano-rolls. His *Cow Cow Blues* is a boogie classic built around a bass line turning up in several other blues. Little Brother Montgomery and Sweet Williams learned it from Cow Cow at Chicago house rent parties.

COOT DAVIS (piano) born probably Miss. Half-brother of 'Monkey Joe', from D'Lo, Miss. Well known around Jackson, Miss., where he had a regular radio programme over WJDX in the 1940s – as Imp (or Emperor) of the Ivories. Played in Atlanta and Memphis. Went to Chicago. Rumoured to have recorded. Taught the *Four O'Clock Blues* to Otis Spann in Jackson (*c.* 1940).

MARTIN DAVIS (piano). Probably still living in Hattiesburg, Miss., in the late 1950s.

MILAS DAVIS (piano) born probably Miss. Played in the Delta in the 1920s. Recorded in St Louis, accompanying blues singers Katherine McDavid (1925) and Missouri Anderson (1926). Went to Chicago *c.* 1930. Still living there in 1968. The *Milas Davis Blues* was learned by Asthma Slim, Little Brother Montgomery, and Sunnyland Slim.

'LITTLE' WILLIE DAVIS (piano) born probably New Orleans, La., *c.* 1906; deceased. Played contests in dance halls with Red Cayou and Baby Brousse. According to Little Sammy: 'He was a blues man.' To Sweet Williams: 'He played everything.' To Tuts Washington: 'He was a variety piano player – used to live down at St Ann and Galvez.' Probably a versatile downtown soloist.

HAROLD 'DUKE' DEJAN (clarinet, alto and tenor saxophone) born New Orleans, La., 4 February 1909. Taught by Lorenzo Tio, Earl Fouché and others. Replaced Lucien Johnson at the College, Inn *c.* 1923. Played with many different bands. Still leading Dejan's Olympia Brass Band in New Orleans in 1970.

CLARENCE DESDUNE (violin, banjo) born New Orleans, La., *c.* 1872; died Ariz., *c.* 1934. Son of bandleader Dan Desdune who went to Omaha, Nebr. Schooled musician. Other members of his Joyland Revelers were Tittytat Steele, Kid Kifer, Gregg Williams (trumpet), Davey Jones, Gene Porter, E. W. Brown (reeds), Vivian (replaced Little Brother Montgomery) (piano), Ransom Knowling Baby Woods (brass and/or string bass), Lucien Barbarin Judge Riley (drums). Cousin Oscar Desdune (piano) took over when Clarence died, according to Brother.

DRIVE 'EM DOWN (piano) died New Orleans, La., probably late 1920s. Legendary blues player in the Battlefield, influenced Champion Jack Dupree whose *Drive 'Em Down Stomp* is a driving, earthy boogie.

ED (drums). Possibly the same person as Eddie Thomas, a drummer of the Bay St Louis area who played there in the bands of Paul Maurice (1920s) and Harry Fairconnetue (after the Depression).

WILLIE EVANS (piano). Remembered by Bubba Brown as having played around Jackson, Miss. Presumably a barrelhouse pianist.

WILL(IE) EZELL (piano, drums, vocal). Blues and ragtime player from the jukes around Shreveport, La. Associated with Elzadie Robinson, a blues singer from the same city. Came to Chicago from Arkansas, according to J. Mayo Williams, and recorded for Paramount from 1926 to 1931. Played anywhere between Detroit and Texas. His *Barrel House Man*, Robinson's *Barrel House Woman* (probably the source of Rambling Thomas's *Saw Mill Moan*) and Lucille Bogan's *Sloppy Drunk Blues* are essentially the same piece, and possibly related to the *Vicksburg Blues*.

HARRY FAIRCONNETUE (banjo, trumpet) born Bay St Louis, Miss., 28 July 1907. Mostly worked around his home town with Paul Maurice (early 1920s), August Saucier (mid-1920s), Buddy Bo

Above left   *Dejan's Olympia Brass Band:* (left to right) *Emanuel Paul, Harold Dejan, New Orleans, 1968.*
Below left   *Dejan's Olympia Brass Band:* (left to right) *Thomas Jefferson, John Smith, New Orleans, 1968.*

Benoit (1930s) and own band. Still living there in 1962. Often played barefoot, according to Judge Riley.

FRIDAY FORD (piano) died possibly *c.* 1940. Probably father of Otis Spann, whom he taught. Presumably a blues man from Belzoni, Miss.

FORD (piano) born possibly New Orleans, La., before 1900. Barrelhouse player from New Orleans. Perhaps the same person as Harrison Ford, a Storyville 'professor'.

LONG TALL FRIDAY (piano) born possibly La., probably 1890s. From Holly Ridge, La., according to Little Brother Montgomery, whom he influenced. Roosevelt Sykes said: 'Friday was one of the first to play *The Forty-Fours*. I didn't meet him, but Lee Green talked about him and showed me, "Friday played it this way".'

PAUL GAYTEN (piano, vocal) born Kentwood, La., 29 January 1920. Son of Little Brother Montgomery's sister Aris Gayten. Brought up in Mississippi. In the mid-1930s, worked with the Don Dunbar orchestra, a touring outfit based in Jackson, Miss. Reported as playing with a local band in summer 1940 – probably the Southland Troubadours. Popular recording artist with own group in New Orleans. Later A&R (Artists and Repertoire) man for Chess, own label Pzazz. Still active in the record business in 1970, probably in Los Angeles.

LEOTHUS (LEE) 'PORKCHOPS' GREEN (piano, vocal) born possibly Miss., *c.* 1900; died *c.* 1945. Blues man from around Vicksburg, Miss. Influenced by Little Brother Montgomery: 'The first time I met Lee Green was in Sondheimer, Louisiana, in 1922. He played in Louise and Valley Park, Mississippi.' Roosevelt Sykes: 'I was on the jazz side before Lee taught me the blues. We travelled together for quite a few years – went for brothers playing in the same town for different people. I first met him in West Helena, Arkansas, in about 1925.' Later operated out of St Louis. Recorded many sides between 1929 and 1937.

GREEN (reeds) died possibly Chicago, Ill. Probably from Baton Rouge, La., according to Little Brother Montgomery. Possibly

Paul Gayten at the height of his popularity.

the same person as Green, a clarinettist in the ERA Band (New Orleans, 1935).

TOMMY GRIFFIN (vocal) born possibly Miss. From Jackson, Miss., according to Little Brother Montgomery: 'Ernest 44 used to play with him.' Also recorded in Memphis (1930).

'CREOLE' GEORGE 'CURLY' GUESNON (banjo, guitar, vocal) born New Orleans, La., 25 May 1907; died New Orleans, 5 May 1968. Excellent musician, played with most of the better New Orleans jazz bands. On tour with F. S. Wolcott's Rabbit Foot Minstrels (mid-1930s). Much recorded with the New Orleans renaissance.

HAINEY (piano). Probably the same person as Ma Hainey, a barrelhouse player around Jackson, Miss., recalled by Bubba Brown.

HOSEA HARRIS (string bass, vocal) born probably New Orleans, La., c. 1905; probably deceased. Played with Kid Howard's kid band in the mid-1920s. Probably went to California. Little Brother Montgomery: 'He was a funny fellow, good talker – used to drink that old moonshine.'

EDDIE HEYWOOD, Sr (piano, trumpet) born probably Ga. (possibly Atlanta), before 1900; probably deceased. Father of pianist Eddie Heywood, Jr, who was born in Atlanta in 1915. Very accomplished pianist with some knowledge of boogie, often recorded for OKeh in the 1920s. At home in Atlanta, New York, and Chicago, but mostly on tour with the vaudeville pair Butterbeans and Susie, usually leading a fine jazz band.

HEZEKIAH (piano) born possibly La., probably 1890s. Was married to Minnie Hicks. Tuts Washington: 'Hezekiah used to be in them tonks where I was bumming around. He could play the hell out of blues – that's all he could play. That was his favourite number, the *44 Blues*. Another fellow around here used to play them same blues, he's named Rocco. I knew him before Hezekiah, and he's the first one I heard playing that – I must have been around sixteen or seventeen years old, he died years ago. I could play them too, it was no singing.' Hezekiah was possibly still alive in New Orleans in 1968.

MINNIE HICKS (vocal) born c. 1898; died probably Chicago, Ill., 1967.

HICKS (guitar) born possibly Ala., probably 1890s. Still living in Chicago in 1968.

HERMAN HILL (piano) deceased. Lived in Summit, Miss., possibly influenced Joe Montgomery.

'LITTLE' SAMMY HOPKINS (piano) born Plaquemine Parish, La., 3 December 1917. Came to New Orleans in the early 1930s and started playing piano, solo and in jazz bands. Made private recordings with Kid Howard in 1937. Often met Fats Domino in the 1940s: 'Fats made it up on his own.' Recorded in the mid-1960s. His *After Hours* is an outstanding example of New Orleans blues 'after hours'. Hearing this piece, Little Brother Montgomery asked, 'Yancey?'. Typical barrelhouse player, also in his band work. His brother Joe played the same kind of music, probably better.

Little Sammy, Beauregard (once Congo) Square, New Orleans, 1968.

WALTER 'LITTLE DOOKY' HOWARD (piano) born possibly New Orleans, La., c. 1907; died probably Cal., probably after World War II. Tuts Washington: 'He was a good piano player that came along in my time, played on the order of me. After he went to the army he settled in California.' Probably a tonk pianist in New Orleans.

CLARENCE 'DUKE' HUDDLESTON (saxophone) born probably Jackson, Miss., after 1903. Own band with Joe White (drums) in the early 1940s. Probably recorded in Jackson for Trumpet in the 1950s. Living in Dallas, Texas, in 1968, according to Butch Roseby.

'IVORY' JOE HUNTER (piano, vocal) born Kirbyville, Tex., 1914. 'Practically all of my ten brothers played piano, or if not, they played drums. They played all over Texas, but never became known as I did.' Joe ran away from home and appeared in carnival shows. Went to California and became popular after World War II as writer and performer of what he calls 'blues ballads'. Probably still active in 1970.

'NEW ORLEANS' TOMMY JACKSON (piano, drums) probably born New Orleans, La., 1890s. Cousin of Tony Jackson, the great New Orleans pianist. Often seen in the Battlefield. Played drums in Fess Manetta's band during World War I at Fort Pike, Ark. (?). Was drafted from Greenville, Miss., replaced by Baby Lovett. Met by Roosevelt Sykes in Vicksburg, Miss. (mid-1920s) and St Louis (mid-1940s). One of 'the best real piano players', according to Little Brother Montgomery. Obviously a very accomplished pianist. Still living in St Louis in 1967.

WALTER JACOBS (VINSON) (guitar, violin, vocal) born probably Miss. (possibly Bolton), c. 1900. Cousin of the Carter brothers, raised together with them. In the early 1920s, associated with Rube Lacy, Tommy Johnson, Ishmon Bracey, Charlie McCoy in Jackson, Miss. Member of the Mississippi Sheiks, made many records all over the country (1928–36, 1961). Probably still alive in Chicago in 1970.

NEHEMIAH 'SKIP' JAMES (guitar, piano, vocal) born near Bentonia, Miss., 9 June 1902; died Philadelphia, Pa., 3 October 1969. Best-known exponent of a strong blues tradition in Bentonia. Took up piano while working in an Arkansas sawmill, inspired by barrelhouse pianist Will Crabtree. Unique, unpianistic style. Superb recording session in 1931, rediscovered in 1964. Influenced Johnnie Temple.

ERNEST '44 FLUNKEY' JOHNSON (piano) born possibly Miss., *c.* 1903. Cousin of Dehlco Robert. According to Little Brother Montgomery: 'His home was at Durant, Mississippi. He wasn't a singer – sometimes I would sing with him. We called him 44 Flunkey because he could play *The Forty-Fours* so good and he was flunking on the Y&MV Railroad. He was terrific.' Went to St Louis in the late 1930s, was in Chicago after World War II. Still living there in 1960. On some of his slower, non-boogie blues sounds like Brother, as do Lee Green, Big Boy Knox, and the unknown pianist who recorded with Arthur Pettis (Chicago, 1930).

LUCIEN (LU) JOHNSON (clarinet, alto saxophone) born probably New Orleans, La., *c.* 1905; died Cal., *c.* 1963. Mostly on the road, e.g. with Don Albert's Trio (1925), Zach Jefferson's band of Baton Rouge, La. (mid-1920s), Joe White, and own band, the Californians (early 1930s).

'DEHLCO' ROBERT JOHNSON (piano, violin) born probably 1890s; died Jackson, Miss., *c.* 1925. According to Little Brother Montgomery: 'He fell dead at the railroad station in Jackson, the

Illinois Central Station in Jackson, Mississippi, 1968.

Illinois Central Station – it was from heart-trouble. His home was at Canton, Mississippi. He played in Wisner, Louisiana.' Influenced Little Brother Montgomery and probably Ernest Johnson, his cousin.

'OLD MAN' CLARENCE M. JONES (piano) born probably 1880s; died c. 1930s. Jelly Roll Morton knew him 'in the early days around Chicago' (probably c. 1910) and influenced him. Jones, a very skilled pianist and orchestrator, was very active there during the 1920s. Led a theatre orchestra, mostly at the Owl Theater, in 1927–8 with Louis Armstrong (trumpet) and Zutty Singleton (drums). Broadcast over WBCN in the mid-1920s, was staff pianist for Imperial, a piano-roll firm. Recorded as soloist, bandleader, and blues accompanist. Later was in Detroit.

HENRY 'POPS' KIMBALL (string and brass bass) born New Orleans, La., 24 March 1878; died New Orleans c. 1932. Father of Narvin Kimball (banjo, string bass). Respected reading musician, played with John Robichaux's society orchestra for a long period. Later mainly in touring bands and on riverboats. Recorded with Fate Morable's (sic) Society Syncopators (New Orleans, 1924). In the Desdune band replaced by Ransom Knowling. Taught bass player Pops Foster.

RALPH LAURENT (violin) born probably La. (possibly New Orleans), c. 1885.

GEORGE LEWIS (GEORGE LOUIS FRANCIS ZENO) (clarinet) born New Orleans, La., 13 July 1900; died New Orleans, 31 December 1968. Outstanding figure of the New Orleans renaissance, great jazz player in the 'folk' idiom. Played with most of the hot bands in New Orleans in the 1920s. Possibly recorded with Lee Collins (trumpet), Tink Baptiste (piano), Alex Scott (string bass), and Roy Evans (drums) (presumably as Imperial Serenaders, New Orleans, 1925). Made countless recordings after 1942.

JOE LEWIS (piano). From Hammond, La., according to Little Brother Montgomery.

MEADE ANDERSON 'LUX(EMBOURG)' LEWIS (piano) born Louisville, Ky., 1905; near Minneapolis, Minn., 7 June 1964. Self-taught blues man, inspired by Jimmy Yancey. Influenced by Cripple

Clarence Lofton, associated with Albert Ammons and Pinetop Smith in Chicago. First recorded there in 1927. Became famous in the late 1930s as powerful boogie pianist.

STEVE J. LEWIS (piano) born New Orleans, La., 19 March 1896; died New Orleans, 1939. Excellent jazz musician, influenced by Fred Washington, taught Joe Robichaux. Played with Sidney Bechet, King Oliver, Johnny Dodds, Zutty Singleton, and others. Worked in Storyville, society orchestras, and barrelhouses. Recorded with Piron's New Orleans Orchestra (New York, New Orleans, 1923–4), Lela Bolden, Willie Jackson, and possibly Dorothy Everetts (New Orleans, 1920s). Made at least one piano-roll. Brilliant execution, advanced harmonies.

WALTER LEWIS, Jr (piano) born Prairieville, La., 21 September 1914. 'I was taking music in school, used to play all that long-hair stuff. But on the outside, man, I'd barrelhouse. Brother didn't fool with no music, just like Tuts – he was mostly ear. That's what the guys liked me for because I could read.' Just a teenager, Walter started playing throughout the South in local bands (Tuts Johnson, Kid Dimes, Claiborne Williams) and tonks, sometimes with blues singer and entertainer Champion Jack Dupree. Took part in many recording sessions, e.g. with B. B. King (Los Angeles, mid-1950s). Still playing, comparatively progressive, in New Orleans in 1970.

HOWARD LOACH (trumpet) born Jackson, Miss., 13 February 1909. Schooled player and arranger. In Chicago, joined Les Wilcox's orchestra in 1934. Gigged with Nat Coles, played with King Kolax (1936), toured with Ruth Ellington (1937). In the late 1930s, working at weekends with own six-piece combo, the Windy City Stompers. Still living in Chicago in 1970.

'CRIPPLE' CLARENCE LOFTON (piano, vocal) born Kingsport, Tenn., 28 March 1886; died Chicago, Ill., 9 January 1957. Extraordinary blues man in Chicago, where he came early in this century. Started recording in the late 1920s. Influenced Meade Lux Lewis and John Mayall with his highly unacademic boogie playing.

ALBERT 'SUNNYLAND SLIM' LUANDREW (piano, vocal) born Vance, Miss., 5 September 1907. Delta blues player working in jukes in Mississippi and Arkansas. Moved to Memphis in the late 1920s;

after World War I in Chicago, where started his recording career. For a period associated with New Orleans pianist Steady Roll Johnson, Lonnie's brother. Still active in Chicago in 1970.

GEORGE ALFRED 'LITTLE GUT' MCCULLUM, Jr (trumpet) born New Orleans, La., 22 February 1906; died New Orleans, 21 March 1938. The third in a row of trumpet-playing George McCullums. Taught by his father and Joe Howard. Played in brass bands and dance halls. Powerful, a better reader than 'get-off man'.

CHARLIE MAHORNER (piano). From around Oakdale, La., according to Little Brother Montgomery. Presumably a barrelhouse player.

FATE MARABLE (piano) born Paducah, Ky., 2 December 1890; died St Louis, Mo., 16 January 1947. Started working on the Streckfus riverboats *c.* 1906, first solo, then with a growing group. Although he used numerous coloured jazz men from New Orleans and St Louis between the wars, his band had to play straight most of the time. Recorded in New Orleans, 1924.

JOE MARTIN (piano, vocal) died McGehee, Ark., *c.* Christmas 1922. From around McGehee and Arkansas City, Ark., according to Little Brother Montgomery. Influenced Brother. Sounds like a New Orleans musician as his *Chinese Man Blues* has a sentimental Creole touch and the *Joe Martin Blues* a 'Spanish' bass – given that Brother's versions are fairly accurate.

JOE MONTGOMERY (piano) born Kentwood, La., 17 May 1909. Mostly stayed with his family. Knew Sudan Washington and Herman Hill around Norfield, Miss., where he played with Henry Ross (drums). Was drafted when in Canton, Miss. In Chicago after World War II. Recorded there with J. B. Lenoir between 1954 and 1960. Influenced Otis Spann. More of a blues man than his brother Eurreal. Still living in Chicago in 1970.

TOLLIE 'DUKE' MONTGOMERY (piano) born Kentwood, La., *c.* 1915. Brother of Joe and Little Brother, uncle of Paul Gayten. Recorded with Brother in 1969 while living in Indiana. Not a professional musician.

DAN MOODY (trombone, string bass) born Mandeville, La., *c.* 1890; died New Orleans, La., June 1959. Popular bandleader in eastern Louisiana after World War I.

Joe Montgomery at his place in South Prairie Ave., Chicago, 1968.

FERDINAND JOSEPH (FERD) 'JELLY ROLL' MORTON (LaMENTHE) (piano, vocal) born New Orleans, La., 20 September 1885; died Los Angeles, Cal., 10 July 1941. One of the greatest personalities of early jazz, first important arranger. Confined to stylish music in high-class Storyville brothels, but in the Battlefield, 'Jelly would sit there and play that barrelhouse music all night – blues and such as that', said Little Barrelhouse Bunkie Johnson, who often played cornet with him. 'He'd play and sing the blues till way up in the day.' Recreated some of the 'low-down' blues and boogies he heard uptown for the Library of Congress (Washington, 1937). Recalled Buddy Bertrand, Josky Adams, Black Butts, Buddy Carter, and other New Orleans tonk pianists, admired Tony Jackson. Anticipated Earl Hines's 'trumpet' style – like Steve Lewis and Teddy Weatherford, who spent his formative years in New Orleans.

POREE NOLAN (piano) born probably 1880s; died possibly New Orleans, La. Storyville professor. From Magnolia, Miss., according to Little Brother Montgomery. Remembered by Tuts Washington.

JOHN HENRY 'JACK' PALMER (piano) born Augusta, Ga., 28 September 1901. Great stride pianist with classical training, forgotten composer of hits like *Everybody Loves My Baby*, *I've Found A New Baby*, *Sweet Emmalina*, *Got Everything*, *Bimbo*, and *Silver Dollar*. Raised in Philadelphia, Pa. Went to New York, was impressed by James P. Johnson and Fats Waller. Own group with Ocie (trumpet), Tricky Sam Nanton (trombone), Elmer Williams (tenor saxophone), and Emmett McKeever (drums). Claimed to have recorded with Joe Jordan's Ten Sharps and Flats and Margaret Johnson (New York, 1926). Went to Chicago in the late 1920s; played there at the Savoy Ballroom with Walter Barnes's band in 1931. Still teaching music in Chicago in 1970.

PAPA LORD GOD (piano). New Orleans barrelhouse player. Little Brother Montgomery's version of the *Papa Lord God Blues* has the 'Spanish' tinge.

LEONARD PARKER (trumpet) born probably La. Seems to have led the band at Slidell, La., with few changes in personnel for several years. Later went to Tyler, Tex., *c.* 1933 where he taught Money Johnson.

DOC PARMLEY (trumpet) born Conway, S.C., 5 April 1905; died Jackson, Miss., *c.* April, 1963. Brother of Luke, married to Irene Wiley. Outstanding minstrel musician. Luke said: 'He had an understanding'.

EDMOND 'LUKE' PARMLEY (various valve instruments) born Conway, S.C., 28 September 1903. Nearly always together with his brother (Doc), when they travelled with tent shows, and after they settled in Jackson, Miss. Still living there in 1968.

Luke Parmley in front of his cafe, Jackson, Mississippi, 1968.

THOMAS AUGUSTUS (GUS) PERRYMAN (piano) born possibly Hattiesburg, Miss., c. 1901. Reading pianist with a style described as 'a nicely balanced diet of clean ragtime, down-home boogie, and a rocking stride piano'. First job with Kid Ory in Mississippi, c. 1917. In the early or mid-1920s played with Gene Crooke's Synco Six in Helena, Ark. Played with Sam Morgan's band (presumably around Hattiesburg) and in a St Louis orchestra under Floyd Campbell (late 1920s) and Harvey Lankford (early 1930s). Settled in St Louis and joined Singleton Palmer's Dixieland Six (1950). Recorded with Palmer. Probably still active there in 1970.

JOSEPH 'BUDDY' PETIT (CRAWFORD) (cornet) born New Orleans, La., 1887; died New Orleans, 4 July 1931. Jelly Roll Morton commented: 'One of the greatest hot cornets that ever lived.' Played with an amazing string of remarkable clarinettists: Sidney Bechet, Jimmie Noone, Albert Nicholas, Barney Bigard, Ed Hall, George Lewis, and Johnny Handy. Made no commercial recordings.

WALTER 'FATS' PICHON (piano, vocal) born New Orleans, La., c. 1905; died Chicago, Ill., 26 February 1967. Studied music, but was often found in barrelhouses and jazz bands. Went to New York and recorded there under his own name and with King Oliver, Luis Russell, Fess Williams, and Fats Waller (1929–30). In the 1930s, led a band touring with Mamie Smith and playing on riverboats. Later cocktail pianist in New Orleans. Versatile musician and arranger.

REESE (piano) deceased. Juke player from York, Ala., according to Big Joe Williams.

RIP TOP (piano). From New Orleans, according to Little Brother Montgomery who played the *Rip Top Blues* with a 'Spanish' left hand.

JOSEPH (JOE) 'JOE DRAG(GER)' ROBICHAUX, Jr (piano) born New Orleans, La., 8 March 1900; died New Orleans, 17 January 1965. Eccentric jazz pianist with barrelhouse background. Taught and influenced by Steve Lewis, learned from Game Kid, associated with Red Cayou. Played in various New Orleans bands in the 1920s, had own swing outfit in the 1930s, accompanied blues singers after World War II, joined George Lewis' band in 1956. Made several recordings, e.g. with Christina Gray, the Jones and Collins Astoria Hot Eight (New Orleans, 1929), own band (New York, 1933; New Orleans, 1936), probably Smiley Lewis (New Orleans, 1954). Reminiscent of Earl Hines. Nephew of bandleader John Robichaux, cousin of tonk pianist Snaggletooth Kelly.

JOHN 'BRICK' ROSEBY (alto saxophone) born Lexington, Miss., 14 February 1910. Cousin of Ed and Butch Roseby. Went to Jackson, Miss., in the mid-1920s and started playing there. With Joe White c. 1930. Stayed with the Southland Troubadours under Doc Parmley's leadership. In the late 1940s to Chicago where he was still gigging in 1968.

RAS 'BUTCH' ROSEBY (trombone, drums) born Lexington, Miss., 28 June 1904. Brother of Ed (banjo), cousin of Brick Roseby (alto saxophone). Raised in Lexington, moved to Jackson, Miss., c. 1929. After having played in Joe White's group, the Roseby brothers formed a band, probably with Man Henderson (trumpet). Butch apparently sat in with the Southland Troubadours. Left Jackson in the mid-1930s to join Chester Lane's Yellow Jackets in Little Rock, Ark. Then in the bands of Joe Robichaux, Papa Celestin, Fats Pichon, and Sidney Desvigne. Returned to Jackson with the war, leading Butch's Band since then. Switched to drums in c. 1950, recorded with Elmore James and Sonny Boy Williamson II for Trumpet (Jackson, early 1950s). Still living there in 1968.

HENRY ROSS (drums) born probably La. (possibly New Orleans). Recorded with Jeter-Pillars Club Plantation Orchestra (St Louis, 1937). Possibly the same person as Henry Russ (drums, trumpet, string bass) who says he played with Little Brother Montgomery. Russ was born in New Orleans, 7 August 1903. Still living there in 1969.

BURNELL SANTIAGO (piano) born New Orleans, La., September 1915; died New Orleans, mid-1940s. Nephew of Willie Santiago (guitar), brother of Blackie Santiago (piano). 'He was a genius' – hardly anybody settled for a lesser attribute when talking about him. Child prodigy, always willing to enter a contest. Made a private recording, *Deep In The Heart Of Texas*, in the early 1940s. Rarely worked in groups, mostly solo for his own amusement.

'STIFF ARM' EDDIE SCOTT (piano) born possibly Ark., according to Little Brother Montgomery. Roosevelt Sykes said: 'I knew Stiff Arm Eddie around Vicksburg, Mississippi in about 1927, and I met him in Elaine, Arkansas. He played *The Forty-Fours*.' Had a brother named Charlie, also a barrelhouse pianist.

CHARLES (CHARLIE, CHUCK) SEGAR (piano, trumpet, vocal) born probably West Louisiana, *c*. 1904. Cousin of Little Brother Montgomery. From Monroe (Sweet Williams) or Lake Charles, La. (Brother). Once married to Nellie Lutcher (piano, vocal) from Lake Charles. Played with King Oliver whose *Mule Face Blues* he mastered, according to Sweet who knew him in Chicago. Recorded there between 1934 and 1940. Seen in Pensacola, Fla. (1920s?), playing piano and trumpet simultaneously. Excellent blues and firm boogie pianist, but the skilled use of a stride bass suggests a jazz musician rather than a limited blues man. Still alive in the 1960s.

'BLIND JUG' SHAW (piano). Travelled and played with New Orleans trumpeter Lee Collins in Alabama in the early 1920s. Possibly the same Shaw who played piano with Thomas Benton's Seven Black Aces, another touring New Orleans band, in the late 1920s.

SKINNY HEAD PETE (piano) born *c*. 1880s. Jelly Roll Morton met him in the first decade of this century: 'My system was to use the piano as a decoy. I'd get a job at one of those honky-tonks along the Gulf Coast, playing piano, then some local boys who called themselves good would ask me to play a game of pool. My system was different from most of the piano players I met along the coast – Skinny Head Pete and Florida Sam, they didn't work because they were kept up by women.'

CLARENCE 'PINETOP' SMITH (piano, vocal) born Troy, Ala., 11 June 1904; died Chicago, Ill., 14 March 1929. Perhaps the most influential one-tune player. Smooth execution, little melodic material – if his recorded output is an indication of his abilities. Started around Birmingham, Ala., then touring with blues singers and vaudeville acts. Played in Mid western cities – in brothels and tonks. Well known at Chicago rent parties. *Pine Top's Boogie Woogie* christened the whole idiom. Little Brother Montgomery employed its piano part for Minnie Hicks' *Monkey Man Blues*.

SNEED (piano). Possibly the same person as Baby Sneed whom Roosevelt Sykes knew in Helena, Ark. (probably early 1920s), of whom he said, 'He was a pretty good blues player'.

ALLEN SNODGRASS (trumpet). On Mid western tour with the 'Stepping Along' show in 1923. The band also included Eugene Watts (trombone).

CHARLIE SPAND (piano, vocal). Possibly from Mississippi. Genuine blues man, often seen in Chicago and Detroit during the Depression. Recorded then, and again in 1940. Rumoured alive in California in the 1960s.

OTIS SPANN (FORD) (piano). Born Belzoni (Jackson?), Miss., 21 March 1930; died Chicago, Ill., 24 April 1970. Little Brother Montgomery: 'Friday Ford is Otis Spann's father. Frank Euston Spann – Old Man Spann married Otis's mother when Otis was quite old. His real name is Otis Ford.' The influence of Brother and Joe Montgomery and possibly Sunnyland Slim is evident in their rippling and rocking work with rhythm and blues bands. Greatest exponent of blues piano in 1970. After World War II in Chicago, associated with Muddy Waters, his half-brother.

JESSE STEELE (alto saxophone). From Arkansas, according to Little Brother Montgomery.

CHARLES '44 CHARLEY' TAYLOR (piano, vocal). From Mississippi (Little Brother Montgomery) or Louisiana between Kentwood and New Orleans (Ishmon Bracey). Played the *44 Blues* around Jackson, Miss., in the 1930s. Recorded in Grafton, Wis., in 1930 – solo or accompanying Bracey and Tommy Johnson. His blues style consists of wild hammering in the right hand against a sliding bass. Unrestrained ragtime player.

JOHNNIE TEMPLE (vocal, guitar) born Canton, Miss., 17 October 1908; died Jackson, Miss., 22 November 1968. Moved to Jackson c. 1920, learned guitar from his step-father, Slim Duckett. Borrowed many songs from Skip James with whom he lived and played in Jackson before he went to Chicago in the early 1930s. First recorded there in 1935, became popular blues singer. Associated with the Harlem Hamfats, a 'swing blues' group mainly composed of musicians from Jackson and New Orleans.

GEORGE W(ASHINGTON) THOMAS (piano, cornet, saxophones, vocal) born probably Houston, Tex., probably 1880s; died Washington, D.C., 1937. Brother of Sippie Wallace (vocal, piano) and Hersal (piano), father of Hociel Thomas (vocal, piano). Primarily a composer. His *New Orleans Hop Scop Blues* as played by Clarence Williams' Blue Five (New York, 1923) is one of the very first recorded documents of boogie.

HERSAL THOMAS (piano) born Houston, Tex., *c*. 1908; died 1928–9. Influenced Albert Ammons who thought Hersal was the first person to bring *The Fives* to Chicago. Cut some records and piano-rolls, like his brother George. Accomplished blues player.

NATHANIEL (NAT) TOWLES (string bass, trumpet) born New Orleans, La., 10 August 1905; died Berkeley, Cal., January 1963. Led famed but unrecorded big band. Started in New Orleans combinations.

TROMBONE RED (trombone). Probably the same person as Robert Freemen (trombone) who recorded as Trombone Red and with Butterbeans and Susie (New York, 1930–1). Freemen played in Eddie Heywood's band with Doc Parmley (cornet) in Georgia, 1926: With the 'Tell 'Em About Me' show in 1928. A trombonist with the same nickname was member of Bebe Ridgley's orchestra (New Orleans, late 1920s).

ANN (ANNIE) TURNER (vocal, piano) born New Orleans, La., 4 July 1921. 'My learning to sing was a gift and also my playing, although it was cultivated by different teachers as my father was an outstanding preacher. He was pastoring several churches and was against my singing the blues as I started out very young – fifteen years of age. I was raised in several cities as my father was travelling most of the time, but I was raised to womanhood in Illinois.' In 1969, she was active in gospel music in Chicago.

COONEY VAUGHN (piano, vocal, trombone) born possibly Barto, Miss., possibly *c*. 1900; died possibly Laurel, Miss., possibly mid-1950s. Big Joe Williams said: 'Cooney was a right-hand man. He played blues and real music. He had a band with Nap Hayes from Tupelo, Mississippi, on guitar.' According to Luke Parmley: 'He played for himself around Jackson – he could juke them folks

Annie Turner, Chicago, summer 1969.

awhile.' Roosevelt Holts: 'He played in Magnolia and McComb, Mississippi and Bogalusa, Louisiana – mostly McComb. He started on organ.' Lee Collins: 'Cooney never left the South, always stayed around Hattiesburg. He was a piano player from his heart and could also fake a little trombone.' In 1920-1, Collins led a band in Hattiesburg, Miss., with Vaughn (trombone), Ed Hall (clarinet), and Jug Shaw (piano). Cooney recorded there in 1936. The Mississippi Jook Band sides (with the gospel duo Blind Roosevelt and Uaroy Graves) feature his exciting hot piano, which is reminiscent of Octave Crosby and Arizona Dranes. His solo recordings remain unissued, so one can only wonder if *Out West Blues* could be the Bob Morton number. In Cooney's *Trembling Blues* Little Brother Montgomery plays semi-quavers in the right hand, again suggesting strong jazz inflections.

RUBEN WALKER (piano) born *c.* 1904. Roosevelt Sykes said: 'He was great – played in Helena, Arkansas.' Champion Jack Dupree remembered going to rent parties in Chicago with Pinetop Smith, Fisher, and a pianist called Ruben. Walker recorded with blues singer Evelyn Brickey (St Louis, 1925). Solid blues piano, partly within the St Louis school (Henry Brown, Peetie Wheatstraw, Walter Davis, Wesley Wallace, Buck McFarland, Stump Johnson, Sylvester Palmor, and others).

ISIDORE '(RED) TUTS' 'PAPA YELLOW' WASHINGTON (piano) born New Orleans, La., 24 January 1907. Versatile player with great knowledge of the blues underground in New Orleans. Associated with Red Cayou, started playing at 'fish fries' and in tonks. Later in local jazz bands. After World War II in California and St Louis. Recorded with Smiley Lewis (New Orleans, 1950-2). Still active in New Orleans in 1970.

LEON 'SUDAN' WASHINGTON (piano) born *c.* 1903; deceased. From McComb, Miss. Ise Youngblood: 'I used to meet him in Columbia, Mississippi.' Little Brother Montgomery said: 'He was a great and wonderful jazz piano player.' Rumoured to have recorded in New Orleans.

EUGENE WATTS (trombone) born possibly Miss. Still alive in Chicago in 1968.

JOSEPH SAMUEL (JOE) WHITE (drums) born Vicksburg, Miss., 4 April 1880. Jelly Roll Morton classed him among the best drummers he knew in his early days. Perhaps they worked for the same minstrel show. White was a star of the Rabbit Foot Minstrels for decades. Was raised in Jackson, Miss., where he was still alive in 1968.

ARNOLD 'DOC' WILEY (piano, vocal) born *c.* 1900. From Helena, Ark., base for other pianists like Roosevelt Sykes, Jesse Bell, Baby Sneed, Willie Kelly, and Joe Crump. Brother of Irene Wiley, brother-in-law of Doc Parmley. Went to Chicago in the late 1920s. Made his first recordings there and led a group with New Orleans drummer Frankie Franko in Indiana, 1929. Was in Detroit, recorded again after World War II. Good ragtime player, full of surprises on the blues, excellent technician. Associated with Sweet Williams during his Chicago period.

FRANK 'SWEET' WILLIAMS (piano) born New Orleans, La., 8 June 1906. Fine New Orleans musician, fascinating blues man. Started playing at 'fish fries' *c.* 1918. Later in a trio with Chris Kelly (cornet) and Papa Crutches (drums). Moved to Chicago in the mid-1920s. Continued working in small New Orleans groups, e.g. with Lee Collins and Herb Morand. During the 1930s, formed a team with Papa Charlie Jackson, a blues singer and banjoist from New Orleans, who died in 1938. Sweet and Little Brother Montgomery took part in the Yancey session for Atlantic (Chicago, 1951), but their recordings were not released. Still living in Chicago in 1968.

JOSEPH LEE 'POOR JOE' 'BIG JOE' WILLIAMS (guitar, vocal) born Crawford, Miss., 16 October 1903. Living monument of the rambling blues man. Still a superb performer. Led a most colourful life. His prolific recording career began in 1935. Sometimes he was backed by comparatively sophisticated musicians. Ransom Knowling to his wife: 'I got to get drunk, Vi – I'm going to play with Big Joe.'

Over page   *Smiley Lewis and his group:* (left to right) *Smiley Lewis, Herman Seale, Tuts Washington, El Morocco Club, Bourbon St. and Iberville St., New Orleans, 1949.*

Sweet Williams at Malizias, North Cicero Ave., Chicago, 1954.

NOLAN 'SHINE' WILLIAMS (drums) born New Orleans, La., *c.* 1902. Played in the bands of Tom Albert (early 1920s), Sam Morgan (1926–7), and Polo Barnes (early 1930s). Recorded with Morgan (New Orleans, spring 1927). Reported still alive in 1959.

UDELL WILSON (piano) born possibly Kansas City, Mo., probably 1890s; died possibly Kansas City, *c.* 1928. From Kansas City where Pete Johnson heard him playing 'a primitive sort of boogie'. Went to New Orleans before the closing of Storyville, worked with many now illustrious jazz men. Played at William Faulkner's favourite place. Respected musician.

JIMMY 'PAPA' YANCEY (piano, vocal) born Chicago, Ill., 1894; died Chicago, 17 September 1951. Outstanding blues player, never a professional. When he left vaudeville in the 1910s to stay in Chicago for good, Tony Jackson and Jelly Roll Morton from New Orleans were the pianists to hear. This could explain his affection for the 'Spanish tinge'. Married to blues singer Mama Yancey, who still lives in Chicago in 1970.

GEORGE 'SON' YOUNG (piano) died Waterproof, La., *c.* 1920s–1930s. From Dumas, Ark., according to Little Brother Montgomery, who was influenced by him.

ISAAC (ISE) YOUNGBLOOD (vocal, guitar, piano) born Tylertown, Miss., 1912. Strong performer in the style of his uncle, Tommy Johnson (guitar). Also plays some boogie piano. Still living in 1970.

Left to right *Little Brother Montgomery, Tollie Montgomery and Jeanne Carroll, Chicago, 1969.*

Lyrics

Transcriptions of Little Brother's songs as shown in the Discography.

NO SPECIAL RIDER BLUES
(Paramount 13006)

Now rider, rider, rider,
   mama, where you been so long?
Now rider, rider, rider,
   Lord, where you been so long?
I ain't had no loving,
   mama, since you been gone.

And I hate, hate to hear,
   hear the little Katy when she blow.
Lord, I hate to hear
   the little Katy when she blow.
Puts me on a wander,
   mama, makes me wanna go.

I can't see, see no train,
   can't hear no whistle blow.
Lord, I can't see no train,
   either hear no whistle blow.
Now it keeps me wondering
   I'm the one (that you adore?).

Now mama, I ain't
   got no plumb good rider now.
Lord, I ain't
   got no plumb good rider now.
Now it seem like my rider
   trying to quit me anyhow.

Now the big bell, the bell is ringing
   and the little bell sadly tone.
Lord, the big bell's ringing,
   the little bell she sadly tone.
Mama, and I'm lonely, lonely, lone',
   a long, long ways from home.

Going to get up, get up in the morning,
   mama, and I ain't gon' say a word.
Going to get up in the morning,
   Lord, ain't gon' say a word.
Going to eat my breakfast
   and sneak to Hattiesburg.

Lord, I know you
   gonna miss me when I'm gone,
Lord, I know you
   gonna miss me when I'm gone,
Gonna miss your baby
   from rolling in your arms.

VICKSBURG BLUES
(Paramount 13006)

I got those Vicksburg blues and
   I'll sing 'em anywhere I go.
I got those Vicksburg blues and
   I'll sing 'em anywhere I go.
Now the reason I sing 'em:
   My baby said she don't want me no more.

I got those Vicksburg blues and
   I'll sing 'em anywhere I please.
I got those Vicksburg blues and
   I'll sing 'em anywhere I please.
Now the reason I sing 'em:
   to give my poor heart some ease.

Now mama, I ain't gon' be your lowdown dog no more.

And I don't like this old place,
  mama,
Lord, and I never will,
And I don't like this old place,
  mama,
Lord, and I never will,
'Cause I can sit right here
  and look at Vicksburg on the
    hill.

LOUISIANA BLUES
(Melotone M12548)

I was born in Fresno
  by the big rock county jail.
Aaaaah,
  by the big rock county jail.
I did not have nobody,
  mama, to go my bond and bail.

Louuuuuisiana
  where I long to be,
Louuuuuisiana
  where I long to be,
I got a cool kind pretty mama
  waiting there for me.

Now mama, I'm going back,
  back to the Lone Star state,
Aaaaah,
  back to the Lone Star state.
(   ), pretty mama,
  I swear you can't make me late.

Now the big bell keeps on ringing
  and the little bell she sadly
    tones.
Aaaaah,
  the little bell she sadly tones.
Mama, I'm lonely, lonely, lonely,
  and I'm long, long ways from
    home.

Now mama, this old place
  don't seem like home to me.
Aaaaah,
  don't seem like home to me.
That's why I'm so worried,
  mama, heartbroken as I can be.

FRISCO HI-BALL BLUES
(Melotone M12548)

Now the Frisco Frisco Hi-Balls
  and the Santa Fé sits still and
    groans.
Now the Frisco Hi-Balls,
  Santa Fé sits still and groans.
I don't like this old place,
  mama, and ain't gonna be here
    long.

Oakdale, Oakdale's on the
    mountain
  and it's Cravens on the Santa Fé
Oakdale's on the mountain,
  Cravens on the Santa Fé,
And I'm going to DeRidder
  and catch the longest train I see.

Now the woman, the woman I
    love,
  mama, she's so far away.
Now the woman I love,
  mama, she's so far away,
And the one I hate,
  I seen her every day.

She got a hand, hand full of
    diamonds
  and her mouth chock full of
    gold,
She got a hand full of diamonds
  and her mouth chock full of
    gold,
And every time she smiles,
  mama, it makes my blood run
    cold.

Lord, I wonder:
  Do she ever call my name?

Lord, I wonder:
    Do she ever call my name?
'If you like me, pretty papa,
    I swear you would feel the same.'

LAKE SHORE BLUES
(unissued)

Green Diamond blowing her whistle,
    train's coming round the trail.
Green Diamond blowing her whistle,
    train's coming round the trail.
I can't ride Pullman,
    guess I'll have to ride the rail.

Chicago, Chicago,
    that is the town for me.
Chicago, Chicago,
    that is the town for me.
Drop me off on the Lake Front,
    that's where I'll be contented to be.

Oooooey hooooey,
    I'm just dreaming dreams.
Oooooey hooooey,
    I'm just dreaming dreams.
The whole world is mine.
    things are not like they seem.

THE WOMAN I LOVE BLUES (Bluebird B6140)

The woman I love
    she's just sixteen years of age,
The woman I love she's
    only sixteen years of age,
And she's a full-grown woman,
    but she just got childish ways.

She got her hands full of diamonds
    and her mouth chock plumb full of gold,
She got a hand full of diamonds
    and a mouth chock full of gold,
And every time she smiles,
    Lord, it makes my blood run cold.

And she's low and she's squatty
    and made right on the ground,
Now she's low and she's squatty
    and made right on the ground,
And she's tailor-made,
    Lord, and ain't no hand-me-down.

And the woman I love,
    Lord, she do not pay me no mind,
Now the woman I love, Lord,
    she don't pay me no mind,
And the one I hate,
    I see her all the time.

And the woman I love
    she's so far away,
The woman I love
    she's so far away,
And the one I hate,
    I see her everyday.

PLEADING BLUES
(Bluebird B6140)

Folks, you don't know
    how worried and bothered I be.
Folks, you don't know
    how worried and bothered I be.
Nobody knows
    but the good Lord and me.

Lord, Lord,
    now won't you hear my plea?

Lordy, Lord,
   now won't you hear my plea?
Now won't you stop my gal
   from mistreating me?

Lord, I'm down on my knees.
   I want you to hear my pleas.
I'm feeling sad today.
   Please, drive these blues away!
My gal have quit me cold.
   So now I'm getting old.
My heart is troubling on.
   I won't be worried long.
Please, send a gat to me
   to ease my misery!

Lord, Lord,
   now I ain't got a friend.
Lordy, Lord,
   now I ain't got a friend.
Now one gal is in jail,
   the other one is in the pen.

VICKSBURG BLUES NO. 2 (Bluebird B6072)

I been worried all day, mama,
   and couldn't hardly sleep last night.
I been worried all day, mama,
   and couldn't hardly sleep last night.
I had the blues for Vicksburg, Mississippi
   and couldn't be satisfied.

Down there is Vicksburg, Mississippi
   where I long to be
Down there is Vicksburg, Mississippi
   where I long to be.
I've got a cool kind pretty mama
   waiting there for me.

Now there is nothing I can do, mama,
   or no more I can say.
There is nothing I can do, mama,
   or no more I can say.
All I know I do in Vicksburg,
   Lord, this very day.

MAMA YOU DON'T MEAN ME NO GOOD (Bluebird 6072)

Now mama, you been hanging out on me.
   I can easily see
There surely must be something going on wrong.
   You stays out all night long.
I can see the change in you.
   How come you do me like you do?
There ain't no need to dog me around
   just because that I'm wild about you.

I love you, mama,
   but you don't mean me no good.
I done everything for you.
   sweet mama, that I could.
I bought you clothes and diamond rings,
   give you all my money and everything.
But still it seems
   that you don't care for me.

If you don't want me, mama,
   now let your daddy be.
Someday I may find
   someone that cares for me.
I ain't no doctor, I can't ease your pain,
   ain't no break-man, I can't change your train.

I love you, mama,
  but you don't mean me no good.

If you don't want me, mama,
  now let your daddy be.
Someday I may find
  someone that cares for me.
You know, sweet, I'm a
      good-looking brown.
  What it takes to please them all –
    I carry it around.
I love you, mama,
  but you really don't mean me
      no good.

MISLED BLUES (Bluebird
    B7806)

Now I left my home, baby,
  honey, just to be with you,
And I left my home, darling,
  baby, just to be with you,
And you left me here, baby,
  and that's the way you do.

Now my mother told me,
  and my father too,
Now my mother told me,
  and my father too,
'Say some good-looking woman
  really gon' be the death of you.'

But I love you, baby,
  and I'll tell the world I do,
I love you, baby,
  and I'll tell the world I do,
And I hope someday, mama,
  you will come to love me too.

Now my mother's dead,
  and my father too.
Now my mother's dead,
  and my father too.
Now I ain't got nobody
  to tell my troubles to.

THE FIRST TIME I MET
    YOU (Bluebird B6766)

The first time I met the blues,
      mama,
  they came walking through the
      wood,
The first time I met the blues,
      baby,
  they came walking through the
      wood.
They stopped at my house first,
      mama,
  and done me all the harm they
      could.

Now the blues got at me, Lord,
  and run me from tree to tree.
Now the blues got at me
  and run me from tree to tree.
You should have heard me
      begging:
  'Mister Blues, don't murder
      me!'

Good morning, Blues!
  What are you doing here so
      soon?
Good morning, Blues!
  What are you doing here so
      soon?
You be's with me in the morning,
  Lord, and every night and noon.

The blues came down my alley,
  mama, and stopped right at my
      door.
The blues came down the alley
  and stopped right at my door.
They gave me more hard luck and
      trouble
  'an I ever had before.

A. & V. RAILROAD BLUES
(Bluebird B6811)

Get your water here,
   baby, and coal where I got
      mine,
Get your water here,
   baby, coal where I got mine,
Get your water here, mama,
   and coal in the 'Bama mine.

Now when you want to, want to
      ride easy,
   now baby, catch the A and V.
Now when you want to ride easy,
   why not catch the A and V?
That's where you pay for your
      riding
   and, Lord, get your free.

Now I hate, hate to hear
   that A and V whistle when she
      blows,
And I hate to hear
   that A and V whistle when it
      blows.
It puts me on a wander,
   mama, makes me want to go.

Now I thought I, thought I heard
   that A and V whistle when she
      blow,
And I thought I heard
   that A and V whistle when she
      blow.
Now it makes me lonesome
   and makes me wanna go.

TANTALIZING BLUES
(Bluebird B6766)

Now the stars really are shining.
   And don't the clouds look
      awful grey?
Now the stars really are shining.
   Don't the clouds look awful
      grey?
I believe the tantalizing blues and
      trouble
   is gonna follow me to my grave.

I'm a poor little boy,
   my baby treats me like a slave,
I'm a poor little boy,
   my baby treats me like a slave,
And I have the tantalizing blues,
      mama,
   Lord, 'most each and every day.

Now have you ever been sad and
      lonely
   and did not know what to do?
Have you ever been sad and lonely
   and didn't know what to do?
And did not have nobody, Lord,
   to tell your troubles to?

The blues will awake you at night,
      mama,
   and worry you the whole day
      through,
The blues will awake you at night,
      mama,
   and worry you the whole day
      through.
And I got those blues so bad,
      mama,
   until I don't know really what
      to do.

VICKSBURG BLUES – PART 3
(Bluebird B6697)

Got a cool loving mama,
   and they calls her Jessie P,
I've got a cool loving mama,
   and they call her Jessie P,
And she's the sweetest woman
   has ever walked down
      Mulberry Street.

Now she's a kind loving baby
and give any man a thrill.
Now she's a kind loving baby
and give any man a thrill.
Now the reason I love her:
She live at Vicksburg on the
hill.

And I would love her, I love her,
and I always will.
And I would love her, I love her,
and I always will.
The reason I love her:
I think of Vicksburg on the hill.

LOUISIANA BLUES –PART 2
(Bluebird B6697)

Now boys, I'm leaving town
because I'm awful blue.
I'm leaving town
because I'm awful blue.
I'll make the Great Northern
(escort?),
baby, out from here to Bogalu'.

Because I'm going down in
Louisiana
where I can have my fun,
I'm going down in Louisiana
where I can have my fun.
Now if you don't believe I'm
leaving
wait until morning come!

Now it is all I've got to tell you,
you don't know like me,
Now this is all I've got to tell you,
you don't know like me
Because down in Louisiana,
that's just where I long to be.

Now, and I know my baby,
she's sure gon' jump and shout,
And I know my baby
sure gon' jump and shout

Now when the Northern roll up,
mama,
and I come walking out.

SANTA FÉ BLUES
(Bluebird B6811)

'Dale on the mountain,
Cravens on the Santa Fé,
Oakdale's on the mountain,
Cravens on the Santa Fé,
And it's a long tall Rosie
is the girl I crave to see.

This time tomorrow,
baby, wonder where shall I be.
This time tomorrow
wonder where, where shall I be.
I'll be back on the mountain,
mama, waiting for the Santa Fé.

Eeeeeasy, mama,
baby, be easy as you can be!
Be easy, mama,
mama, be easy as you can be!
Now easy, baby,
until I get back on the Santa Fé.

Now if tomorrow be Sunday,
mama, wonder what will the
next day be.
If tomorrow be Sunday,
mama, what will the next day
be?
It will be Blue Monday,
now my baby's leaving me.

SOMETHING KEEPS A-
WORRYIN' ME (Bluebird
B6658)

Lord,
baby, there is something keep on
worrying me.

Lord,
   there is something keep on
      worrying me.
That's my old-time baby
   has gone back to her used-to-be.

I give her all of my money,
   and she left me cold in hand,
I give her all of my money,
   and she left me cold in hand,
And taking all of my money
   and give it to another man.

Now mama, that's all right,
   baby, that's all right for you.
Now mama, that's all right.
   baby, that's all right for you.
Now mama, that's all right
   most any old way that you do.

Now the sun gon' shine,
   mama, in my back door some
      day.
Now the sun gon' shine
   baby, in my back door some day.
Now the wind's gon' change,
   mama,
   and blow my worried blues
      away.

OUT WEST BLUES
(Bluebird B6916)

I was laying upstairs, mama,
   trying to take my rest,
And a notion struck me,
   Lord, I believe I'll go out west.

Now I'm going out west, mama,
   Lord, and I can't take you,
And I'm going out west, mama,
   baby, and I really can't take you,
Because it's nothing out there,
   mama,
   that a woman like you can do.

In Louisiana,
   man, where I long to be,
Man, I would go to Cravens,
   but I'm afraid of Hardy Gill.
And if Hardy don't get you,
   Sweet Papa surely will.

Just as soon as the train,
   mama, makes up in the yard.
Just as soon as the train, mama,
   baby, makes up in the yard,
And I'm out west bound –
   that's if the bulls don't have me
      barred.

LEAVING TOWN BLUES
(Bluebird B6916)

Now I'm leaving town, baby,
   'cause you know you treats me
      wrong.
And I'm leaving town, baby,
   'cause you know you treat me
      wrong.
You go out at night and get full of
      bad whiskey
   and stay out the whole night
      long.

And I tried everything,
   mama, in this world to get along
      with you,
And I tried everything
   in this world to get along with
      you,
Now, and you know I love you.
   That's why you treat me like
      the way you do.

And I'm going, I'm going,
   mama, and your crying won't make me stay,
And I'm going, I'm going,
   and your crying won't make me stay.
And the more you cry, mama,
   the further that you drive me away.

Now when I leave this town, mama,
   you can pin crêpe on my door.
When I leave this time, mama,
   you can pin crêpe on my door.
And I won't be dead.
   baby, but I ain't coming here no more.

WEST TEXAS BLUES
(Bluebird B7178)

I got a letter from Texas.
   How do you reckon it read?
I got a letter from Texas.
   And how do you reckon it read?
It say, 'Hurry home, Brother,
   for the one you love is dead.'

And I went to the station,
   but the, the train had gone,
And I went to the station,
   but the train had gone.
I got a-thinking about my baby,
   and I started walking on.

And I walked up on a stranger,
   I told him I were in so much misery.
I walked up on a stranger,
   told him I w' in so much misery.
He said, 'You're nearest out to Texas,
   you better catch the T and P.'

And they stop me off in Texas
   in a little place they call San Anton',
And they stop me off in Texas
   in a place they call San Anton',
And you can't really imagine
   how you hear those wild ox moan.

NEVER GO WRONG BLUES
(Bluebird B6825)

Now boys, I once had a good woman,
   but I really did not treat her right,
I once had a good woman,
   but I did not treat her right,
And I would do everything evil
   and everything I could for spite.

I would go out at night
   and get full of bucket gin,
I would go out late at night
   and get full of bucket gin,
And she'd be absolutely hospitable
   if she (had?) even asked me where I had been.

Now I'm sorry that I mistreated her,
   just as sorry as a man can be.
Now I'm sorry I mistreated her,
   just as sorry as a man can be.
Now it seem the more that I do for her
   it is the less she care for me.

Now boys, if you got a good woman
   treat her right in every way,

Now if you got a good woman
   treat her kind in every way
Because a real good woman
   can't be found every day.

SORROWFUL BLUES
(Bluebird B7277)

Now baby, please tell me:
   What make you treat me mean?
Now baby, please tell me:
   What make you treat me mean?
Now you treats me just like
   that I'm someone you've never seen.

And you treat me so bad, baby,
   till I can't hardly sleep at night,
And you treat me so bad, baby,
   till I can't hardly sleep at night,
And it look like everything you do
   you really do it for spite.

But I love you, baby.
   That's why you treat me so.
But I really love you, baby.
   That's why you treat me so.
But I will always love you
   as if you don't want me no more.

Now mama, some old day,
   Lord, some long lonesome day,
Now mama, some old day,
   baby, some long lonesome day
And you really will be sorry
   that you ever treated me this a-way.

MISTREATIN' WOMAN BLUES (Bluebird B7178)

Boys, have you ever had a woman,
   and she didn't mean you no good?
Have you ever had a woman,
   and she didn't mean you no good?
And you trust her with your heart,
   and she treat it just like a piece of wood.

And you will turn your back on everybody,
   baby, who were your best friend,
And you will turn your back on everybody,
   baby, who really were your best friend,
On account of a no-good woman,
   and then she's loving other men.

Then you will sit right down and worry
   about the friends that you could gain.
Then you will sit right down and worry
   about the friends that you could gain.
After you have forsaken everybody
   it will be the 'count of another Jane.

Now boys, don't never let no
   woman treat you nice and kind,
Now boys, don't never let no woman
   treat you nice and kind,
Because she's only (begging?) you.
   I can judge her as I do mine.

CHINESE MAN BLUES
(Bluebird B6658)

Mister Chineeman, Mister Chineeman,
   he walks around all day.

Now Chineeman, Chineeman,
  he smokes his pipe of clay.
He got stuck onto the Chinee girl,
  and these here's the words he replied:
'Hongkong, hoo-oo-oo-oooo,
  all the boys begin to cry,
Hongkong, hoo-oo-oo,
  Hongkong Lou-oo-oo.'
He got stuck on the Chinee girl,
  and these here is the words he replied:
'Won't you open up your door
  and let me in?'

Now Chineeman, yeah yeah-n,
  walks around all day.
Now Chineeman, yeah yeah-n,
  smokes his pipe of clay.
He says to her,
  'Baby, what's the matter with you?'
She say, 'I got those Hongkong
  hug-away, hick-a-way Chinee blues.'

He says to her,
  'Now baby, what's the matter with you?'
She says, 'I got those
  hug-a-way, hick-a-way,
    Chineeman blues.'

Abbreviations

In the Discography and Index the following abbreviations are used:

acc	accompanied	Minn.	Minnesota
accn	accordion	Miss.	Mississippi
Ala.	Alabama	Mo.	Missouri
alt	alto saxophone	Nebr.	Nebraska
Ariz.	Arizona	N.J.	New Jersey
Ark.	Arkansas	org.	organ
Bb	Bluebird	Pa.	Pennsylvania
bbs	brass bass	Pm	Paramount
bjo	banjo	pno	piano
Bwy	Broadway	S.C.	South Carolina
Cal.	California	sax	saxophone
clt	clarinet	sbs	string bass
cnt	cornet	sop	soprano saxophone
dms	drums	tamb	tambourine
Fla.	Florida	tbn	trombone
Ga.	Georgia	ten	tenor saxophone
gtr	guitar	Tenn.	Tennessee
hca	harmonica	Tex.	Texas
Ill.	Illinois	tpt	trumpet
Ky.	Kentucky	uke	ukulele
La.	Louisiana	vcl	vocal
ldr	leader	Vi	RCA-Victor
mand	mandolin	vln	violin
Md.	Maryland	wbd	washboard
Me	Melotone	Wis.	Wisconsin

Discography

This is a list of the sessions before World War II in which Little Brother Montgomery took part. It is based on *Blues and Gospel Records* 1902-42, by W. J. Godrich and R. M. W. Dixon. Only the original issues are shown.

Grafton, Wis., probably autumn 1930:

IRENE SCRUGGS: Vcl acc by Little Brother Montgomery (pno).
L-498-	*Borrowed Love Blues*	Pm 13046
L-500-	*Back To The Wall*	Pm 13046
	Good Meat Grinder	Pm 13023
	Must Get Mine In Front	Pm 13023

Note: Brother recalled that he also recorded *St Louis Woman Blues* with Irene Scruggs.

LITTLE BROTHER MONTGOMERY: Vcl acc by own pno.
| L-501-1 | *No Special Rider Blues* | Pm 13006 |
| L-502-1 | *Vicksburg Blues* | Pm 13006 |

MINNIE HICKS: Vcl acc by Little Brother Montgomery (pno).
| L-514-1 | *Monkey Man Blues* | Bwy 5099 |
| L-515-1 | *Sweet Rider* | Bwy 5099 |

Note: *South Parkway Blues* and *Steel Mill Blues* were previously attributed to Minnie's 1931 session, but it seems more likely that these sides were really made, if at all, for Paramount. Brother also remembered having recorded *Black Boy Blues* with Minnie.

19th floor, American Furniture Mart Building, 666 N. Lake Shore Drive, Chicago, Ill., 5 January 1931:

'E' MONTGOMERY: Vcl acc by own pno; with Hicks (gtr) and Minnie Hicks (comments–1).
| C-6879-A | *Louisiana Blues* –1 | Me M12548 |
| C-6880-B | *Frisco Hi-Ball Blues* | Me M12548 |

MINNIE HICKS: Vcl acc by Little Brother Montgomery (pno) and Hicks (gtr).
| C-6881- | *Sweet Rider Blues* | Me M12549 |
| C-6882- | *Jim Jam Blues* | Me M12549 |

unknown location (Chicago, Ill. ?), possibly 1933:

Little Brother Montgomery (vcl, pno).
        Lake Front Blues   probably Victor test

New Orleans, La., 10 August 1935:

MONKEY JOE: Vcl acc by own pno and Walter Jacobs (gtr).
94414-1	*Sweet Petuna Stomp*	Bb B6061
94415-1	*Gonna Beat It Back To Memphis, Tenn.*	Bb B6061
94416-1	*Monkey Joe Got The Blues*	Bb B6114
94417-1	*Hard Time Blues*	Bb B6114

LITTLE BROTHER MONTGOMERY: Vcl acc by own pno; with Walter Jacobs (gtr–2) and Monkey Joe (comments–3).
94418-1	*The Woman I Love Blues* - 2, 3	Bb B6140
94419-1	*Pleading Blues* - 2, 3	Bb B6140
94420-1	*Vicksburg Blues No. 2*	Bb B6072
94421-1	*Mamma You Don't Mean Me No Good* –3	Bb B6072

HARRY CARTER: Vcl acc by own pno and Walter Jacobs (gtr).
94422-1	*Hoo Doo Blues*	Bb B6095
94423-1	*Smoke-Stack Blues*	Bb B6095
94424-1	*Deep Blue Ocean Blues*	Bb B6210
94425-1	*These Jackson Women Will Not Treat You Right*	Bb B6210

St Charles Hotel, 211 St Charles St., New Orleans, La., 16 October 1936.

TOMMY GRIFFIN: Vcl acc by Ernest 44 (pno) and Walter Jacobs (gtr).
02625-1	*I'm Gonna Try That Meat*	Bb B6696
02626-1	*Young Heifer Blues*	Bb B6734
02627-1	*Hey Hey Blues*	Bb B6734
02628-1	*Dying Sinner Blues – Part 2*	Bb B6834
02629-1	*I'm Gonna Buy Me Some*	Bb B6696
02630-1	*Mistreatin' Papa*	Bb B6872

02631-1	*Miserable Life Blues*	Bb B6793
02632-1	*Snake Hipping Blues*	Bb B6872
02633-1	*Little Tommy Blues*	Bb B6756
02634-1	*On My Way Blues*	Bb B6793
02635-1	*Dying Sinner Blues – Part 1*	Vi unissued
02636-1	*Dream Book Blues*	Bb B6756

ANNIE TURNER: Vcl acc by Little Brother Montgomery (pno) and Walter Jacobs (gtr).

02637-1	*Black Pony Blues*	Bb B6707
02638-1	*Deceived Blues*	Bb B6788
02639-1	*Workhouse Blues*	Bb B6788
02640-1	*Hard On You*	Bb B6707

LITTLE BROTHER: Vcl acc by own pno; or pno solo–4.

02641-1	*Misled Blues*	Bb B7806
02642-1	*The First Time I Met You*	Bb B6766
02643-1	*A. & V. Railroad Blues*	Bb B6811
02644-1	*Tantalizing Blues*	Bb B6766
02645-1	*Vicksburg Blues – Part 3*	Bb B6697
02646-1	*Louisiana Blues – Part 2*	Bb B6697
02647-1	*Santa Fé Blues*	Bb B6811
02648-1	*Something Keeps A-Worrin' Me*	Bb B6658
02649-1	*Out West Blues*	Bb B6916
02650-1	*Leaving Town Blues*	Bb B6916
02651-1	*West Texas Blues*	Bb B7178
02652-1	*Never Go Wrong Blues*	Bb B6825
02653-1	*Sorrowful Blues*	Bb B7277
02654-1	*Mistreatin' Woman Blues*	Bb B7178
02655-1	*Chinese Man Blues*	Bb B6658
02656-1	*Farish Street Jive* –4	Bb B6894
02657-1	*Crescent City Blues* –4	Bb B6733
02658-1	*Shreveport Blues* –4	Bb B6733

CREOLE GEORGE GUESNON: Vcl acc by Little Brother Montgomery (pno).

02659-1	*Goodbye, Good Luck To You*	Bb B6706

WALTER JACOBS: Vcl acc by own gtr and Ernest 44 (pno).

02660-1	*How Did It Happen*	Bb B6673
02661-1	*Rats Been On My Cheese*	Bb B6673

Index

Page numbers in **boldface** indicate a paragraph on that artist in the section 'Who's Who' (in these cases instrumentation is omitted, and full names are not necessarily given). *Italic* page numbers show presence in photographs. Doubtful spellings are followed by (?).

Adams, Josky (pno, vcl) 78
Akers, Garfield (gtr, vcl) 11
Albert, Tom (tpt) 90
Alcorn, Alvin 41, 60, **60**
Alcorn, Oliver 39, *41*, 55, 60, **60**, *61*
Amacker, Frank Lucean (pno, vcl) 24
Ammons, Albert 45, **60**, 75, 84
Ammons, Eugene (Gene) (ten) 60
Anderson, Buster (pno, vcl) 23
Anderson, Missouri (vcl) 65
Anderson, Varnado 17, 18, **60**
Anderson, Willie (pno) 17, 18
Ard (?), Sabato (pno) 29
Armstrong, Louis Daniel 'Satchmo' (tpt, vcl) 23, 74
Asthma (or Piano) Slim (pno) 33, 65

Baptiste, Xavier 'Tink' (pno) 63, 74
Barbarin, Lucien (dms) 67
Barker, Danny 35, *35*, **60**
Barker (Dupont), Louise 'Blue Lu' (vcl) 60
Barnes, Emile (clt) 23
Barnes, Paul D. 'Polo' (reeds) 60, 90
Barnes, Walter (sax) 78
Bascomb, Arthur (pno) 64
Bechet, Sidney (clt, sop, etc.) 75, 80
Bell, 'Red-Eyed' Jesse (pno, vcl) 87
Belton, C. S. (ldr) 51
Bennett, Warren (pno, clt, alt) 39
Benoit, Edgar 'Buddy Bo' (ldr) 67-8
Berry, Odie (dms) 35
Bertrand, Buddy (pno) 78
Bigard, Albany Leon (Barney) (reeds) 80
Bigeou, Esther (vcl) 64
Black Butts (pno) 78
Black Emile *see* Emile Thomas
Black Texas (vcl) 20
Blackmon, Doug 51, **62**
Blind Blake 45, **62**
Blind Homer *see* Bud Hall
Blind Jug *see* Jug Shaw
Bob Alexander *see* Alexander Robinson

Bogan, Lucille (vcl) 67
Bolden, Buddy (dms) 33
Bolden, Charles 'Buddy' (cnt) 23
Bolden, Lela (vcl) 75
Boogus (pno) 23
Box Car 53, **62**
Bracey, Rev Ishmon (gtr, vcl) 9, 72, 83
Brickey, Evelyn (vcl) 86
Briscoe, Nelishi (vcl) 36
Broonzy, William Lee Conley 'Big Bill' (gtr, vcl) 62
Broussard, Albert 'Baby Brousse' (pno, vcl) 65
Brown, Clifford Raymond (Ray) (tpt) 62
Brown, E. W. (clt) 67
Brown, Henry (pno, vcl) 86
Brown, John Henry 'Bubba' (gtr, pno, vcl) 67, 70
Brown, Raymond 39, 40-1, *40-1*, **62**
Brumfield, Leon (pno) 17, 18
Bunch, William 'Peetie Wheatstraw' (pno, gtr, vcl) 86
Burnt Face Jake (pno) 21
Butterbeans & Susie *see* Edwards

Call, Bob 45, **62**
Campbell, Arthur (pno) 24
Campbell, Floyd (dms, vcl) 60, 80
Carrington, Jerome 42, **62**
Carey, Jack (tbn) 63
Carter (Chatmon), Bo (gtr, vln, clt, vcl) 52
Carter, Buddy (pno) 78
Carter, Harry 52, **62**
Carter (Chatmon), Lonnie (vln, vcl) 52
Carter (Chatmon), Sam (gtr, sbs, vcl) 52, 62
Cayou, Red 26, 27, **63**, 65, 80, 86
Celestin, Oscar 'Papa' (tpt, vcl) 51, 60, 81
Charles, Louis (tbn) 51
Chatmon *see* Carter
Chicago Bill (pno) 45
Chinaman Walter (vln) 19
Christian, Narcisse J. 'Buddy' (pno, gtr, bjo) 24
Clayton, Kid 27, **63**
Coates, Freddie 33, **63**
Cohn, Zinky Augustus (pno) 42
Colar, George 27, *28*, **64**
Coleman, Jesse 33, 39, 52, **64**, 65
Cole(s), Nathaniel (Nat) 'King' (pno, vcl) 75

Collins, Lee (tpt) 27, 42, 55, 74, 81, 82, 86, 87
Cook, Ann 27, **64**
Cook, Charles L. 'Doc' (ldr) 62, 63
Cook, Son (pno) 21
Crabtree, Will (pno) 73
Crook, Clarence 'Tompy' (dms) 52
Crooke, Eugene (Gene) (bjo, gtr) 80
Crosby, Octave (pno) 29, 86
Crump, Joe (pno, vcl) 87
Cuga (?), Jackie (pno) 45

Darensbourg, Caffrey (bjo, gtr) 63
Darensbourg, Joe (reeds) 55
Davenport, Cow Cow 45, 62, **64–5**
Davis, Coot 33, 39, 52, 64, **65**
Davis, Martin 29, **65**
Davis, Milas 33, 45, **65**
Davis, Odette (pno) 36
Davis, Walter (pno, vcl) 86
Davis, Willie 27, **65**
Decou, Walter (pno) 60
Dehlco Robert *see* Robert Johnson
Dejan, Harold 39, 40, *40–1*, **65**, 66
Desdune, Clarence 39–41, 67
Desdune, Daniel (Dan) (cnt) 41, 67
Desdune, Oscar (pno) 67
Desvigne, Sidney (tpt) 51, 60, 62, 81
Dickerson, Aletha *see* Aletha Robinson
Dimes, Wesley 'Kid' (tpt) 75
Dixon, Willie (sbs, gtr, vcl) 18, 33
Dodds, Johnny (clt, alt) 75
Dodds, Warren 'Baby' (dms, wbd) 55, 60
Dolton, Wellington (bjo) 36, 60
Dominguez, Paul, Jr. (vln, gtr) 22, 27
Dominique, 'Don' Albert (tpt) 60, 73
Dominique, Anatie F. (Nattie) (tpt) 55
Domino, Antoine 'Fats' (pno, vcl) 71
Don Albert *see* Albert Dominique
Don Dunbar *see* Lawrence Jefferson
Douglas, K.C. (gtr, vcl) 53
Dranes, Arizona Juanita (pno, vcl) 86
Drive 'Em Down 27, **67**
Duckett, Lucien D. 'Slim' (gtr, vcl) 83
Dumaine, Louis (tpt) 64
Dupree, William Thomas 'Champion Jack' (pno, vcl) 67, 75, 86
Durand, Maurice (tpt) 36, 60

Ed 29, **67**
Edwards, Joe 'Butterbeans' (vcl) 45, 70, 84
Edwards, Susie (vcl) 45, 70, 84
Ellington, Ruth (vcl) 75
Emerson, Rosser (alt, ten) 48, 50, 51, **52**
Ernest 44 *see* Ernest Johnson
Esters (?), Willie (pno) 29
Evans, Roy (dms) 74
Evans, Willie 29, **67**
Everetts, Dorothy (vcl) 75

Ezell, Will 31, 45, **67**

Fairconnetue, Harry 39, 40, *40–1*, 67, **67–8**
Fisher (pno) 86
Florida Sam (pno) 82
Flunkey *see* Ernest Johnson
Ford 17, **68**
Ford, Friday 33, **68**
Ford, Harrison (pno) 68
Forty-Five (pno) 45
44 Charley *see* Charley Taylor
44 Flunkey *see* Ernest Johnson
Foster, George Murphy 'Pops' (sbs, bbs) 24, 55, 60, 74
Fouché, Earl (reeds) 39, 65
Framion, Son (pno) 17
Frankie Franko *see* François Mosley
Freeman, Robert 'Trombone Red' (tbn) 84
Frenchman Joe (pno) 29

Game Kid (pno, vcl) 23, 80
Garland, Edward (Ed) 'Montudie' (sbs, bbs) 55
Gayten, Paul 32, 53, **68**, 69, 76
Gibson, Loomis (pno) 17, 18
Goff, Felix (reeds) 39
Graves, 'Blind' Roosevelt (gtr, vcl) 86
Graves, Uaroy (tamb, vcl) 86
Gray, Christina (vcl) 81
Green 29, 35, **68–9**
Green (clt) 69
Green, Lee 20, 33, 68, **68**, 73
Griffin, Tommy 52, **69**
Guesnon, Curly 48, 50, 51, 53, 63, **70**
Guidry, Jeffrey 'Cooney' (pno) 63

Hainey **70**
Hainey, Ma (pno) 33, 70
Hall, Alfred (Fred) 'Tubby' (dms) 55
Hall, Edmond (Ed) (reeds) 80, 86
Hall, 'Blind' Homer 'Bud' (pno) 33
Hall, Minor 'Ram' (dms) 55
Handy, 'Captain' John (Johnny) (clt, alt) 27, 62, 80
Harney, Maylon (?) 'Pet' (gtr) 11
Harney, Richard 'Can' (gtr, pno, vcl) 11
Harp-Blowing Rabbit (hca) 29
Harris, Hosea 29, **70**
Harris, Otis (gtr, vcl) 11
Hawkins, Forrest (vln) 19
Hawkins, Mark (vln) 19, 51
Hayes, Napoleon (Nap) (gtr) 84
Haywood, Ernest (pno) 17
Henderson, George (dms) 36, 60
Henderson, Man (tpt) 51, 81
Hennington, H. T. (bjo, pno) 48, 50, 53
Henry, Oscar 'Chicken' (pno, tbn) 24

Heywood, Eddie, Jr. (pno)   70
Heywood, Eddie, Sr.   45, **70**, 84
Hezekiah   27, **70**
Hicks   45, **70**
Hicks, Edna (vcl)   64
Hicks, Minnie   45, **70**, 82
Hill, Herman   32, 37, **70**, 76
Hines, Earl Kenneth 'Fatha'
  (pno)   42, 78, 81
Holts, Roosevelt (gtr, vcl)   29, 86
Hopkins, Joe (pno)   71
Hopkins, Sammy   27, *28*, 65, *71*, **71**
Howard, Avery 'Kid' (tpt, vcl)   70, 71
Howard, Joe (cnt, bbs)   76
Howard, Walter   27, **72**
Huddleston, Duke   51, **72**
Humphrey, Earl (tbn, sbs)   64
Hunter, Ivory Joe   53, **72**
Hunter, Shep (pno)   32

Jackson, 'Papa' Charlie (bjo, gtr,
  vcl)   33, 87
Jackson, Preston (tbn)   55
Jackson, Tommy   21, 33, 51, **72**
Jackson, Tony (pno, vcl)   72, 78, 91
Jackson, 'New Orleans' Willie (vcl)   75
Jacobs, Walter   9, 52, 64, **72**
James, Elmore (gtr, vcl)   81
James, Sadie (vcl)   63
James, Skip   33, **72–3**, 83
Jaxon, Frankie 'Half Pint' (vcl)   63
Jefferson, Lawrence 'Don Dunbar
  (tpt)   68
Jefferson, Thomas (tpt)   *66*
Jefferson, Zach (ldr)   73
Jeter, James (alt)   51, 81
Johnson, Alonzo (Lonnie) (gtr, pno,
  vln, vcl)   55, 76
Johnson, David Lee (pno)   53
Johnson, Ernest   20, 21, 52, 69, **73**, 74
Johnson, Frank (bjo)   35
Johnson, Harold 'Money' (tpt)   78
Johnson, James 'Steady Roll' (pno, vln,
  gtr, bjo, vcl)   76
Johnson, James 'Stump' (pno, vcl)   86
Johnson, James P(rice) (pno)   78
Johnson, Rev Ledell (gtr, vcl)   9
Johnson, Lucien   39, 48, 65, **73**
Johnson, Margaret (vcl)   78
Johnson, Pete (pno, dms)   60, 91
Johnson, 'Dehlco' Robert   19, 20, 73,
  73–4
Johnson, 'Little' Robert (gtr, hca,
  vcl)   11
Johnson, Tommy (gtr, mand, vcl)   9,
  39, 72, 83, 91
Johnson, Tuts (tpt, etc.)   27, 75
Johnson, William Manuel (Bill) (sbs,
  gtr, bjo, bbs)   55
Johnson, Willie '(Little Barrelhouse)
  Bunk(ie)' (tpt)   17, 78
Jones, Clarence   42, **74**

Jones, David (Davey) (sax, etc.)   67, 81
Jones, 'Little' Johnny (pno, vcl)   52
Jones, Richard 'M(yknee)' (pno, vcl)   24
Jordan, Joe (pno)   78
Jordan, Thomas 'Louis' (clt, sop,
  alt, vcl)   51

Kelly, Chris (tpt)   23, 27, 64, 87
Kelly, George 'Snaggletooth' (pno)   81
Kelly, Guy (tpt, vcl)   36
Kelly, Willie (pno)   87
Kid Sheik *see* George Colar
Kifer (?), Kid (tpt)   67
Kimball, Narvin Henry (bjo, sbs)   74
Kimball, Pops   39, **74**
King Kolax *see* William Little
King, Riley B. 'B(lues) B(oy)' (gtr,
  vcl)   75
Knowling, Ransom (sbs, bbs, dms)   55,
  67, 74, 87
Knox, Big Boy (pno, vcl)   31, 73

Lacy, Ruben (Rube) (gtr, vcl)   9, 72
Lane, Chester (pno)   81
Lankford, Harvey (tbn)   80
Laurent, Ralph   28, 29, **74**
Ledbetter, Huddie 'Leadbelly' (gtr, pno,
  accn, vcl)   11
Lee, George E. (ten)   51
Lemon, Overton 'Smiley Lewis' (gtr, vcl)
  81, 86, *88-9*
Lenoir, J. B. (gtr, hca, vcl)   76
Lewis, George   28, *28*, **74**, 80, 81
Lewis, Joe   19, **74**
Lewis, Meade Lux   45, 60, **74**, 75
Lewis, Steve   24, 27, **75**, 78, 80
Lewis, Walter   13, 24, 27, 31, **75**
Lindsay, John (tbn, sbs, bbs)   55
Little Dooky *see* Walter Howard
Little Low Friday (pno)   39
Little Sammy *see* Sammy Hopkins
Little Willie *see* Willie Davis
Little, William '(King) Kolax' (tpt)   75
Loach, Howard   48, 50, *50*, 51, **75**
Lofton, Cripple Clarence   45, **74-5**, **75**
Longshaw, Fred (pno)   65
Long Tall Friday   19, **68**
Lovett, Sam 'Baby' (dms)   72
Luandrew, Albert   33, *34*, 65, **75**, 83
Lutcher, Nellie (pno, vcl)   82

McCoy, Charles (Charlie) (mand, gtr, vcl)
  9, 72
McCoy, Robert (pno, vcl)   65
McCoy, Wilbur '(Kansas) Joe' (gtr, mand,
  vcl)   9
McCullum, George, Jr.   39, 40-41, *40-1*,
  60, **76**
McCullum, George Alfred, Sr (cnt)   76
McDavid, Katherine C. (vcl)   65

McFarland, '(Barrelhouse) Buck' (pno, vcl) 86
McKeever, Emmett (dms) 78
Maghett, Samuel 'Magic Sam' (gtr, vcl) 55
Mahorner (?), Charlie (pno) 29, **76**
Major, Eddie (pno) 20
Mancy (pno) 20, 21
Manetta, Manuel 'Fess' (pno, etc.) 72
Marable, Fate 27, 74, **76**
Marcell, Bob (mand, vcl) 23
Marcell, Henry (gtr, vcl) 23
Martin, Joe 20, 21, **76**
Maurice, Paul (reeds) 67
Mayall, John (pno, org, gtr, hca, vcl) 75
Miles, Lizzie *see* Lizzie Pajaud
Miller, Percy (pno) 29
Miller, Willie 'Rice' 'Sonny Boy Williamson II' (hca, gtr, vcl) 81
Monkey Joe *see* Jesse Coleman
Montgomery, Bob (pno) 42
Montgomery, Gonzy (various instruments) 17
Montgomery, Joe 17, 32, *32*, 52, 70, 76, **76**, **77**, 83
Montgomery, Leo (pno) 42
Montgomery, Tollie 17, 32, **76**
Moody, Dan 28, 29, 63, **76**
Morand, Herbert (Herb) 'Kid' (tpt, vcl) 87
Morgan, Sam (tpt, vcl) 27, 48, 80, 90
Morganfield, McKinley 'Muddy Waters' (gtr, hca, vcl) 83
Morton, Bob (pno, vcl) 17, 18, 86
Morton, Jelly Roll 10, 17, 23, 24, 27, 42, 63, 65, 74, **77-8**, 80, 82, 87, 91
Mosley, François (Francis) 'Frankie Franko' (dms) 87
Muddy Waters *see* McKinley Morganfield

Nanton, Joseph (Joe) 'Tricky Sam' (tbn) 78
Nash, Lemon (uke, gtr, bjo, vcl) 64
Nelson, Davidson C. (Dave) (tpt, pno) 60
Nelson (Delisle), 'Big Eye' Louis (clt, sbs, bjo, accn) 22, 23, 36
Nicholas, Albert (Al) (reeds) 80
Nicholas, Joseph 'Wooden Joe' (tpt, clt) 27, 64
Nichols, Hyram (ten) 48
No Leg Kenny (pno) 31
Nolan, Poree 27, **78**
Noone, Jimmie (clt) 63, 80

Ocie (Asie Gary ?) (tpt) 78
Oden, James Burke 'St Louis Jimmy' (vcl, pno) 60
Oliver, Joseph (Joe) 'King' (tpt) 75, 80, 82

Ory, Edward 'Kid' (tbn, etc.) 55, 62, 80

Pajaud (Landreaux), Elizabeth Mary 'Lizzie Miles' (vcl, pno) 64
Palmer, Henry 42, **78**
Palmer, Singleton N. 'Cocky' (bbs, sbs) 80
Palmer, Sylvester (pno, vcl) 86
Papa Crutches (dms) 87
Papa Lord God 17, 18, **78**
Papa Sweet (dms) 29
Parenti, Anthony (Tony) (clt) 55
Parker, Leonard 28, **78**
Parker, Willie (pno) 29
Parmley, Doc 45, 48, *50*, 51, 53, 62, **78**, 79, 81, 84, 87
Parmley, Luke 48, *50*, 51, 62, 78, *79*, **79**, 84
Parrish, Avery (pno) 64
Pate, Lamon 'Stuff' (pno) 53
Paul, Emanuel (ten) 66
Payne, Odie (dms) 55
Pearson, Alice (vcl) 63
Peetie Wheatstraw *see* William Bunch
Peg Top 53
Perryman, Gus 33, **80**
Pet & Can *see* Harney
Petit, Buddy 27, 29, 60, 64, **80**
Petti(e)s, Arthur (gtr, vcl) 73
Peyton, David (Dave) (ldr) 63
Piano Slim *see* Asthma Slim
Pichon, Fats 27, 62, **80**, 81
Pillars, Hayes (ten) 51, 81
Piron, Armand J. (vln) 27, 75
Porter, Eugene (Gene) (reeds, tpt) *52*, 67
Prescott (?), B. J. (pno) 32
Purnell, Alton (pno, vcl) 24

Rainey (Pridgett), Gertrude 'Ma' (vcl) 45
Reese 17, **80**
René, Henry 'Kid' (tpt) 27, 64
Rhinehart, Mack (pno, vcl) 65
Ridgley, William (Bill) 'Bébé' (tbn, dms) 84
Riley, Judge Lawrence (dms, sbs, vcl) 40, 67, 68
Rip Top 17, 18, **80**
Robichaux, Joe 27, 60, 75, **80-1**, 81
Robichaux, John (vln, sbs, accn, dms) 74, 81
Robinson (Dickerson), Aletha (pno) 42
Robinson, 'Bob' Alexander (pno, gtr, vcl) 42
Robinson, Elzadie (vcl) 67
Rocco (pno) 70
Roland, Walter 'Alabama Sam' (pno, gtr, vcl) 64
Roseby, Brick 38, 48, *50*, 62, 81, **81**
Roseby, Butch 9, 48, *49*, *52*, 72, 81, **81**
Roseby, Ed (bjo) *52*, 81

Ross, Henry 38, 48, *50*, 51, 52, 76, **81**
Roussell, Bud (sbs, vcl) 23
Rush, Otis (gtr, vcl) 55
Russ, Henry (dms, tpt, sbs) 81
Russell, Luis Carl (pno) 80

St Cyr, John A. (Johnny) (gtr, bjo) 22, 23
St Louis Jimmy *see* James Oden
Santiago, Burnell 27, **81**
Santiago, Lester 'Blackie' (pno) 81
Santiago, Willie (gtr, bjo) 81
Saucier, August (tbn) 67
Saucier, Edgard (sax) 39, 55
Scott, Alex (sbs) 74
Scott, Arthur 'Bud' (gtr, bjo, vcl) 55
Scott, Charlie (pno) 82
Scott, Clarence 'Bud' (mand, vcl) 19
Scott, Eddie 20, **82**
Scruggs, Irene 'Chocolate Brown' (vcl) 45
Seale, Clarence (pno) 17
Seale, Herman (dms) *88–9*
Segar, Charlie 31, **82**
Severe (?), Hanson (pno) 29
Shaw (pno) 82
Shaw, Jug 32, **82**, 86
Singleton, Arthur James 'Zutty' (dms) 63, 74, 75
Skinny Head Pete 21, **82**
Smiley Lewis *see* Overton Lemon
Smith, Elizabeth (Bessie) (vcl) 63
Smith, Jerome 'Porkchop' (dms) 55
Smith, John (dms) 66
Smith (Robinson), Mamie (vcl) 9, 80
Smith, Pinetop 13, 27, 45, 60, 64, 75, **82**, 86
Sneed 45, **83**
Sneed, Baby (pno) 83, 87
Snodgrass, Allen 35, **83**
Sonny Boy Williamson II *see* Rice Miller
Spand, Charlie 45, 62, **83**
Spann, Otis 52, 64, 65, 68, 76, **83**
Steele, Jesse 51, **83**
Steele, Tittytat (tpt) 67
Stiff Arm Eddie *see* Eddie Scott
Stokes, Lucius (sax) 51
Sunnyland Slim *see* Albert Luandrew
Sykes, Roosevelt (pno, vcl) 20, 68, 72, 82, 83, 86, 87

Tate, Erskine (bjo) *62–3*
Taylor, Charley 39, **83**
Temple, Johnnie 33, 64, *73*, **83**
Thomas, Eddie (dms) 67
Thomas, 'Black' Emile (pno) 33
Thomas, George W. 24, 45, 84, **84**
Thomas, Hersal 45, 60, 84, **84**
Thomas, Hociel (vcl, pno) 84
Thomas, Willard 'Rambling' (gtr, vcl) 67

Tio, Lorenzo, Jr. (clt, ten) 63, 65
Tompy *see* Clarence Crook
Toothpick (pno) 45
Towles, Nat 51, **84**
Tremer, George H. (pno) 64
Trombone Red 29, **84**
Turner, Annie 53, **84**, *85*

Vaughn, Cooney 17, 18, 32, 52, **84–6**
Vigne, Jean (pno) 63
Vigne, Manuel (pno) 63
Vinson, Walter *see* Walter Jacobs
Vivian (pno) 67

Walker, Harold (Harry) (gtr) 51
Walker, Ruben 31, 45, **86**
Wallace (Thomas), Beulah 'Sippie' (vcl, pno) 84
Wallace, Wesley (pno) 86
Waller, Thomas (Tom) 'Fats' (pno, org, vcl) 42, 78, 80
Washington, Fred (pno) 24, 75
Washington, Sudan 17, 32, 76, 86
Washington, Tuts 25, *25*, 27, 63, 65, 70, 72, 75, 78, **86**, *88–9*
Watts, Eugene 35, 83, **86**
Weatherford, Teddy (pno) 78
Wells, 'Ragging' Willie (pno) 20
White, Joe 9, 48, 51, *52*, 62, 72, 73, 81, **87**
Wilcox, Leslie (Les) (ten) 75
Wiley, Arnold 45, **87**
Wiley, Irene (vcl) 45, 78, 87
Williams, Claiborne (tpt) 75
Williams, Clarence (pno, jug, vcl) 13, 24, 84
Williams, Elmer (reeds) 78
Williams, Gregg (tpt) 67
Williams, Jabo (pno, vcl) 64
Williams, Joe 12, 30, 62, 80, 84, **87**
Williams, Shine 39, 40, *40–1*, **90**
Williams, Spencer (pno, vcl) 24
Williams, Stanley R. 'Fess' (reeds) 80
Williams, Sweet *43*, *44*, 45, 65, 82, 87, **87**, *90*
Williamson, John Lee 'Sonny Boy' (hca, vcl) 55
Wilson, Theodore (Teddy) (pno) 42
Wilson, Udell 27, **91**
Woodard, J. C. (accn, pno) 51, *52*
Wooden Joe *see* Joe Nicholas
Woods, Baby (bbs) 67
Wynn, Albert (Al) (tbn) 55

Yancey, Estella 'Mama' (vcl) 91
Yancey, Jimmy 17, 45, 60, 71, 74, **91**
Yeager, Johnny (pno) 21
Young, Son 20, **91**
Youngblood, Ise 29, *30*, 86, **91**